Adventure Awaits:

HELPING FAMILIES PREPARE FOR CROSS-CULTURAL LIFE

JENI WARD & KATH WILLIAMS

First Edition 2025

© COPYRIGHT INTERWOVEN 2025

All rights reserved. No part of this publication may be reproduced, stored in or introduced into a Retrieval system; or be transmitted, in any form, or by any means (electronic, mechanical, photocopying, recording or otherwise) without the prior written permission of the publisher. This book is sold, subject to the condition that is shall not by way or trade or otherwise, be lent, resold hired out, or otherwise circulate without the publisher's prior consent, in any form of binding or cover other than that in which it is published and without a similar condition, including this condition, being imposed on the subsequent purchaser.

ISBN paperback: 978-0-6457886-0-0

This edition was published in Aberfoyle Park by Mission Interlink in September 2025

Typesetting by: Kath Williams
Cover layout by: Jeni Ward & Kath Williams

Endorsements

Moving abroad to a new culture can be an overwhelming experience for parents to navigate for themselves and their children, particularly for the first time. It's exciting to consider the adventure of following God's call of moving abroad; yet there are so many unknowns and facets of preparation to consider.

Adventure Awaits is a rich resource that will support the entire family as they begin their journey to live cross-culturally. Adventure Awaits addresses a wide range of important topics that are valuable to consider for such a significant move. Each chapter is full of a variety of ways to learn and prepare including journal prompts, discussion questions, and fun activities to make sure the whole family is cared for and prepared for their adventure.

M. Green, ISV International Resource Person for TCKs and Families

I am so pleased to see this resource become available! 'Adventure Awaits' is a great help for families preparing to transition to global field work, providing good emotionally healthy pre-work and settling in ideas, that will help families thrive.

Analy Alfonso
Pioneers Member Care – Families & TCKs

Moving to another country is a life-changing journey filled with excitement, uncertainty, and countless questions. This thoughtfully curated resource packet is nothing short of a lifeline for families navigating this major transition. It is a warm, practical, and compassionate guide that meets families where they are; offering not just logistical advice, but genuine emotional support. From engaging activities that help children process change, to insightful suggestions for easing cultural adjustments, to practical checklists that ensure nothing is overlooked, this packet provides holistic guidance every step of the way. It's clear that care and intention went into every page.

Megan C. Norton-Newbanks,
author of Belonging Beyond Borders: How Adult Third Culture Kids Can Cultivate a Sense of Belonging

✈ Contents

About Us – 5
Welcome to the Adventure Awaits Workbook – 6

Section 1: TCK Beginnings
Preparing Your Child for the Adventure Ahead – 8
Section 2: Staying Connected
Involving Extended Family in the Journey – 16
Section 3: Where Is Home?
Understanding Identity and Belonging for TCKs – 25
Section 4: All the Feels
Helping Your Family Navigate Emotions in Transition – 33
Section 5: Goodbyes & Grief
Helping Your Family Leave Well – 43
Section 6: Practical Tips for Moving Overseas and Traveling with Children
Packing, Planning, and Travel Prep for Families – 52
Section 7: Entering In
Preparing Your Children for a Move to a New Country – 60
Section 8: Seeing with New Eyes
Helping Your Children Understand Wealth and Poverty in a New Culture – 69
Section 9: Important Questions to Ask Along the Way
Understanding Power Distance, Culture, and Family Expectations – 77
Section 10: Staying Safe
Helping Your Children Feel Secure in a New Culture – 85
Section 11: Navigating Education Overseas
A Practical Guide for Selecting Schooling Options in a Cross-Cultural Context – 93
Section 12: Additional Needs and Neurodiversity
Supporting Your Child's Unique Needs When Preparing to Move Overseas – 110
Section 13: Belonging in Transit
Helping Your Child Define Home – 118
Section 14: Routines & Rhythms
Creating a Sense of Stability – 125
Section 15: Language & Communication
Building Bridges Before the Move – 132
Section 16: Faith & Spiritual Formation in Transition
Guiding Your Children Spiritually Through Change – 135
Section 17: Debriefing and Planning for Home Assignments
Reflecting and Preparing for the Next Season – 137
Section 18: Bonus Tools
Practical Printables, Checklists, and Family Conversation Cards – 139
Section 19: Resources
Books, Websites, and Further Support – 149

INTERWOVEN

Interwoven is a Missions Interlink Ministry, created through a partnership of dedicated workers with a passion for nurturing Third Culture Kids, ensuring their physical, spiritual, and mental well-being on the field. Our primary mission is to develop resources that directly engage Third Culture Kids. Additionally, we aim to support and provide valuable resources to those who work with and care for them.

KATH WILLIAMS

Kath is a dedicated and professional social worker with a profound passion for supporting Third Culture Kids (TCKs) in their growth and development. Currently, she works with TCKs through two mission organizations in Australia. Kath is the co-author of "Navigating a Global Transition Again: A Journey of Faith" and "Thongs or Flip Flops: A Book for Aussie TCKs."

With 20 years of experience working with children and teens, Kath's diverse background includes work with Indigenous communities, foster children, and community camp-sites. She spent two years in Cambodia, where she contributed to the student support team at Hope International School and volunteered with middle and high school students at a local international church youth group.

Outside of her professional life, Kath enjoys going out for coffee and food with friends, exploring with her camera, visiting zoos, reading, listening to music, and traveling as much as she can.

JENI WARD

Jeni Ward is a Third Culture Kid (TCK) whose journey has taken her across diverse landscapes including Ethiopia, South Sudan, Canada, and Australia. With over 13 years of experience in cross-cultural ministry, Jeni has dedicated her life to understanding and bridging the gaps between different cultures. As a lifelong learner, she is passionate about walking alongside other TCKs, offering guidance, support, and a deep sense of community.

As a founding member of Interwoven, an organization dedicated to developing materials and resources for TCKs (and the producer of this book). Through her work with Interwoven, she has been instrumental in creating resources that address the unique challenges and opportunities that come with a multicultural upbringing. These include God in the Mess and God in the Cracks. As well as co-authoring "Navigating a Global Transition Again: A Journey of Faith" All this together with Kath Williams. Check these great resources out at https://www.interwovenglobal.com .

Her commitment to this cause reflects not just in her professional life, but also in her everyday interactions, where she continuously seeks to connect, inspire, and empower those around her through coaching and debriefing.

Welcome to the Adventure Awaits: Workbook

This workbook is here to support you every step of the way as you prepare your family, especially your children, for the exciting journey of living abroad. Moving can bring both challenges and wonderful opportunities, whether it's your first time or your fifth. Use this space to reflect, plan, and work through everything together, making your transition smoother and more meaningful.

You'll discover pages designed for both parents and children, making it easy for everyone to get involved. Each chapter aligns with the topics in the Family Guide and features journal prompts, conversation starters, and fun activities to encourage your family to connect and engage with what's ahead.

This isn't just a workbook to get through quickly. You might find it helpful to take your time, perhaps exploring one chapter a week or focusing on the sections that resonate most with your family's current needs. Feel free to personalise the activities to match your children's ages, personalities, and learning styles, making the experience even more meaningful and enjoyable.

As you write, draw, and talk together, may this workbook serve as a reminder:
✨ You are not alone.
🌍 Your story is valuable.
🏡 And home can be many places.

🛠️ How to Use It

Each section in this guide is structured with consistency to make it easy for you to use week by week or adapt to your own pace. Every section includes:
- Overview & Purpose: A clear explanation of why this topic matters for preparing well
- Parent Learning: Foundational concepts and examples drawn from TCK and family transition literature
- Practical Tools & Strategies: Real-world activities, models, and tips to help you apply what you're learning
- Parent Reflection Task: Questions to help you explore your own beliefs, habits, and past experiences
- Family Task: A creative, hands-on activity designed to help your family connect and explore the topic together
- Companion Journal Page: Prompts and open-ended space for your children to draw, write, paste photos, or reflect in their own words
- Key Takeaways Summary: A bite-sized recap to highlight what's most important in this section

You can work through the chapters individually, as a family, or in a group setting. The activities are designed to be flexible—use what suits your family best and skip or adapt anything as needed.

🔖 Creating a Companion Journal for Each Child

While this workbook provides shared family activities, we encourage you to help each of your children create their own Companion Journal. These pages are included throughout the workbook to help them reflect, draw, and express themselves in their own way. You can print extra copies of the journal pages or let your children design their own creative journal using a scrapbook, sketchpad, or notebook.

This personal journal becomes a treasured keepsake—capturing their thoughts, memories, and questions as they prepare to step into a new culture. It's also a powerful tool for self-expression, emotional processing, and building a sense of identity that will travel with them.

👪 Who It's For

This workbook is created for:
- Parents preparing to take their children overseas for cross-cultural work
- Children of all ages (with parents adapting activities to suit their development)
- Families wanting to navigate transition with emotional intelligence and spiritual awareness.
- Ministry teams are looking for tools to support TCKs and their caregiver.s

It's designed to help the family feel seen, heard, and prepared for the road ahead.

⌛ Suggestions for Pacing

This workbook is not meant to be completed in one sitting. We recommend:
- Focusing on one chapter per week in the months leading up to your departure
- Using the family tasks and activities to prompt deeper discussion and shared reflection
- Revisiting sections during transition moments—like packing, arrival, or early adjustment
- Keeping it accessible during the move and return as a place to process change over time

There's no perfect pace— move at the rhythm that fits your family's season.

Section 1:

TCK Beginnings
– Preparing Your Child for the Adventure Ahead

 Overview

Recognising the importance of preventive care can really support your kids as they adapt to new environments.

"Healthy TCKs have had preventive care throughout their lives, and so they've developed benefits that have been deliberately and lovingly drawn from each challenge."
— Lauren Wells, Raising Up a Generation of Healthy Third Culture Kids (2020), p.15

As the people who are closest to your child, you hold a special and important role in helping them prepare for life overseas. Just being with you is wonderful, but children, whether they're young or older, really thrive when they feel confident in sharing their thoughts and being listened to. This warmth and support help them flourish in new and unfamiliar environments, making their journey exciting and full of growth.

Let's embark on this journey as a family. Giving yourself ample preparation now helps create a foundation of resilience, openness, and emotional well-being that will support you in the months and years to come.

What is a Third Culture Kid (TCK)?

As your family gets ready to live overseas, you'll likely hear the term "Third Culture Kid"—but what does it mean?

Third Culture Kids (TCKs) spend a big chunk of their childhood in a culture that's different from their parents' homeland. This often happens when people work internationally in areas like mission work, global business, diplomacy, or humanitarian roles.

TCKs grow up surrounded by different cultures, creating a unique blend that combines elements from all the places they've lived. This leads to rich experiences and strengths, including:
- Understanding across Cultures
- Being adaptable
- Having empathy and resilience

However, it can also bring challenges, such as:
- Uncertainty about who you are
- Troubles with feeling like you fit in
- Dealing with the pain of saying goodbye often

By understanding what it means to be a TCK, your child can start to develop a positive sense of identity around their globally mobile life.

Why This Section Matters

Children move through more than just physical change—they also go through emotional, spiritual, relational, and cultural shifts. When they receive support and feel understood, they're more likely to navigate the challenges of transition with confidence and resilience, rather than feeling overwhelmed.

This section is about beginning well—with emotional safety, self-awareness, and a sense of belonging.

👨‍👩‍👧 Parent Task: Creating an Emotionally Safe Space

💡 Why it matters:

Preparing your kids for an overseas move is more than just passports and packing lists. Emotional preparation is foundational. As Lauren Wells reminds us in Raising a Generation of Healthy Third Culture Kids: "Healthy TCKs have had preventive care throughout their lives, and so they've developed benefits that have been deliberately and lovingly drawn from each challenge." Your role in creating a safe, emotionally supportive environment will impact how your kids adjust and thrive.

What to Do:

Reflect Together
- Set aside 30–60 minutes for relaxed, one-on-one time with each child this week. Use drawing, play, or storytelling to open space for emotional conversations. Let them lead.

Listen Well
- Practice active listening is about giving someone your full attention, making eye contact, and showing you care. Don't jump in to try and fix or dismiss how they're feeling. Sometimes, just being there and being present is the most healing thing you can do.

Observe Individual Needs
Every child is different. Ask yourself:
- Who needs routine to feel grounded?
- Who uses words to express themselves? Who uses actions?
- Who may need extra physical reassurance (like hugs or closeness)?
- Who thrives on one-on-one connection?

Set a Weekly Check-In
Create a family ritual of checking in once a week. Each person shares:
- One thing they're excited about
- One thing they're nervous about
- One thing they're curious about

Make it fun—use a talking stick, draw a "feelings monster," or make it part of a Sunday evening snack time.

📝 Reflect and Plan

Questions to Consider:

What does a "safe and supportive space" look like in your home?

How do your children best communicate their feelings?

What family rhythms could help you stay connected through this transition?

Write your reflections below:

Child 1:
 Needs, concerns, or strengths:

Child 2:
 Needs, concerns, or strengths:

Child 3:
 Needs, concerns, or strengths:

Ideas for family rituals or check-ins:

👪 Family Task: "This is Me" Identity Page

This activity helps your children reflect on who they are before the move—anchoring their sense of self as they enter new places and cultures.

Instructions:
- Each family member takes a blank sheet or enters into their companion page
- Outline something that represents you (e.g., a book, a soccer ball, a tree, or even a backpack).

Inside the outline, fill the space with words, drawings, or symbols that represent:
- Interests
- Hobbies
- Personality traits
- Special memories or relationships

Share your creation with the family.

Take a photo of each page and keep a digital or printed copy. You'll revisit these during the adjustment period overseas.

📖 Companion Activity Ideas

ALL ABOUT ME

My name is _____

I am _____ years old.

I live.... _____

I go to ..... (school, Kindy) _____

I am in....(Grade) _____

My Self Portrait!

My Friends are

1. _____

2. _____

3. _____

4. _____

5. _____

My favourite food is:

Adventure Awaits

✅ **Key Takeaways for Parents:**

- Children are watching how you prepare and process.
- Starting emotional conversations early builds trust and resilience.
- Identity formation begins before you arrive overseas.
- Creating connection through rituals and reflection empowers your child's journey.

Section 2:

Staying Connected
– Involving Extended Family in the Journey

🌍 Overview

As you prepare for your international move, it's easy to focus on the logistics and emotional needs within your immediate household—but the ripple effects extend much further. Grandparents, aunties, uncles, and close family friends often feel the shift deeply, even though they aren't the ones boarding the plane.

Involving extended family early can help everyone feel seen, valued, and included. It also strengthens your children's identity and connection to their roots. A move overseas doesn't need to mean disconnection—it can be an opportunity to build even deeper, more intentional relationships across distance.

Why Involving Extended Family Matters

- It Strengthens Your Child's Sense of Belonging

Those who keep in touch with their wider family are reassured they're loved – no matter where they call home. These connections help strengthen their sense of identity and bring a sense of continuity during a time of change.

- It Acknowledges the Grief and Change for Everyone

Grandparents might miss regular visits, while siblings or close friends may feel left out. By recognising this impact, you foster open discussions and show you care about everyone's feelings.

- It Builds a Supportive Foundation

When your extended family understands why you're going and feels included in your plans, they're more likely to support you in prayer, encouragement, and practical help from a distance.

- It Models Intentional Relationships

Your kids are learning to stay connected—even when they're apart. Keeping in touch with family members teaches them how to nurture relationships in a thoughtful and creative way.

👨‍👩‍👧‍👦 Parent Task: Communicating the Journey and Building Connection

💡 Why it matters:

Prepping your extended family for your move overseas boosts your kids' support network and lightens the emotional load for everyone involved. It's not just about sharing info – it's about inviting others to join your family on this journey.

What to Do:

- Share Your "Why"

Set aside time to chat with grandparents and close relatives about your calling, hopes, and motivations for going abroad. Share your feelings, not just your plans.

- Invite Their Input

Ask how they feel about the move. What are their worries? What would help them stay connected? This opens space for relationships, not just reactions.

- Build Connection Rhythms

Create a plan for regular catch-ups. Will it be weekly video chats? Monthly letters? Birthday packages? Set rhythms that work for both time zones and emotional needs.

- Equip Them with Tools

Make sure your relatives are comfortable with the technology they need to stay in touch. Offer to walk them through Zoom, WhatsApp, or shared photo albums.

📝 Reflect and Plan

Questions to Consider:

How do our extended family members feel about our move?

What rhythms of connection could we begin before we leave?

What does each child need from their wider family during this transition?

Write your reflections below:
Family Member 1:
 Concerns / Ideas for connection:

Family Member 2:
 Concerns / Ideas for connection:

Ideas for check-in rhythms or shared traditions:

Write your reflections below:
Family Member 1:
 Concerns / Ideas for connection:

Family Member 2:
 Concerns / Ideas for connection:

Ideas for check-in rhythms or shared traditions:

👨‍👩‍👧 Family Task: Create a "Staying Connected Plan" Together

Work as a family to make a visual or written plan for staying connected with loved ones.

Instructions:

- Draw a Connection Map – In the centre, place your family. Around you, add circles for grandparents, aunts/uncles, cousins, and friends.

- Add Connection Ideas – Next to each name, list 1–2 ways your family plans to stay in touch (e.g., video call every Sunday, send a birthday card, share photos).

- Make it Fun – Use stickers, drawings, or symbols to represent different ways of staying in touch.

- Post It Up – Keep it on the fridge or in a journal as a reminder of the people who love you from afar.

Companion Activity Ideas

People I will miss the most are:

Things I want to tell Grandma/Grandpa before we go

Supporting Grandparents Through the Transition

Grandparents often go through a tough time when they decide to move overseas, feeling grief, confusion or guilt. However, they can also become a source of strength and stability for your children. Here are some ways to support them:

Practical Ideas:

- Have an Honest Chat – Make time for them to share their feelings. Acknowledge the loss they're facing and really listen
- Teach the Tech – Help them use Face-time, Messenger, or shared albums.
- Create Shared Activities – Try video bedtime stories, movie nights, or prayer together.
- Send Updates – Share photos, drawings, or voice messages regularly.
- Plan Visits – Involve them in dreaming and planning for future reunions.
- Send Keepsakes – Mail small crafts or care packages as reminders of your bond.
- Grandparent dates- Create Grandparent dates before they go away with each child

✅Key Takeaways for Parents:

- Extended family are part of your support system—even from afar.
- Open, honest communication helps everyone adjust.
- Kids thrive when their connections are maintained, not cut off.
- It's never too early to build healthy rhythms of long-distance relationships

Section 3:

Where Is Home? Understanding Identity and Belonging for TCKs

🌍 Overview

As you prepare your children for life overseas, one of the most profound themes you'll encounter is identity—who your child is, where they belong, and how they define "home." For Third Culture Kids (TCKs), identity is shaped by family and faith and by a blend of cultures, places, and experiences that often stretch across continents.

Helping children explore their sense of self—and where they feel "at home"—equips them with tools to manage change, hold onto their values, and confidently embrace their multicultural journey.

The Changing Meaning of "Home"

Traditionally, home is considered one place—where you were born or raised. However, for TCKs, the concept is more complex. "Home" might not be a single location, but rather:
- The smell of food from one country
- A grandparent's house in another
- The friends they've left behind
- The family routines that stay the same across cultures

As one little girl said during a transition workshop after sculpting her "home" out of clay: "Wherever we move or wherever my family is, that is where home is for me."
Children benefit from knowing that home can be more than one place. It's okay to say, "I have three homes," or "I'm not sure where I belong right now." Naming that ambiguity helps them feel safe in the uncertainty.

The Role of the Passport Country

Understanding and maintaining a connection to their passport country gives children an anchor amid global mobility. This country often provides a reference point for legal identity, cultural values, and long-term educational or career pathways.
Helping your children connect with their passport country can:
- Give them a sense of cultural continuity
- Strengthen family identity and heritage.
- Ease transitions during visits or home assignments.
- Offer them language, traditions, and social cues that many of their peers back "home" may share.

> **Why This Chapter Matters**
> When children are given time, space, and language to explore their identity, they develop a more secure sense of self. This is especially important when they encounter questions like:
> - "Where are you from?"
> - "Why do you talk like that?"
> - "Why don't you know this game/trend/TV show?"
>
> TCKs who understand their complex identity and can express it confidently are more likely to embrace the beauty of who they are and extend that understanding to others

👪 Parent Task: Carrying Culture Forward

💡 Why it matters:

Your family's cultural traditions, language, and lifestyle habits from your passport country are essential identity markers for your children. Continuing them overseas—whether it's Friday night pizza, ANZAC Day traditions, or bedtime prayers in your native language—helps your child remain grounded and connected to their roots.

What to Do:

- **Reflect Together**

Take time as parents to discuss what routines or cultural practices matter to you. Which ones do you want to continue? Which ones might need to adapt?

- **Choose a Few Anchor Traditions**

Pick 3 5 simple traditions or routines you'll prioritise during the first six months on the field. These could include:
- Celebrating holidays from your passport country
- Cooking familiar meals once a week
- Sharing family stories or songs from home

- **Discuss with Your Children**

Let your kids have a say. What do they want to carry with them from "home"? Their answers may surprise you!

✏️ Reflect and Plan

Questions to Consider:
What traditions or routines represent our home culture?

Which parts of our family identity do we want to keep strong while overseas?

What does each child value most about life in our passport country?

Write your reflections below:
Child 1:
 Traditions or routines to carry forward:

Child 2:
 Traditions or routines to carry forward:

Child 3:
 Traditions or routines to carry forward:

Ideas for family cultural connection while overseas:

👨‍👩‍👧 Family Task: Creating a Transition Scrapbook for Your Child's Journey

Keep building on your child's Companion Journal by creating a physical or digital scrapbook together. A simple ring binder with plastic sleeves works well and allows you to add pages over time. This evolving memory book becomes a valuable tool to support your child's emotional journey through transition.

Suggested Sections:

👨‍👩‍👧 Family Members
- Photos of grandparents, cousins, and extended family
- Names, birthdays, and fun facts

🎈 Special Places
- Take a "farewell tour" of your current home
- Photograph favourite parks, bedrooms, or hangouts
- Add captions or drawings about what makes them special

🏡 Future Home (if known)
- Include pictures of your new country or house
- Add maps, flags, or facts to create anticipation and familiarity

💌 Letters from Loved Ones
- Ask friends and family to write notes or draw pictures
- Add envelopes or taped-in letters that your child can revisit on tough days

Companion Activity Ideas

What does home feel like to me?

If I could take five things from my home with me, I'd take...

A tradition I want to keep doing is...

✅ Key Takeaways for Parents:

- Home is more than a location—help your child name the people, places, and routines that define "home" for them.
- Connecting to the passport country helps your child build an anchored identity amid mobility.
- A sense of belonging grows through intentional traditions, storytelling, and ongoing reflection.

Section 4:

All the Feels – Helping Your Family Navigate Emotions in Transition

 Overview

Before you focus on your kids' emotional needs, take a moment to ask yourself:
- How are you going?

This season is full of goodbyes, packing lists, excitement, grief, and uncertainty. Every part of it affects how you show up for your family. Whether you recharge through time alone or social connection, your emotional well-being matters deeply in this journey.

Your children are watching. Your ability to name and regulate your emotions teaches them how to do the same. The more supported and steady you feel, the more equipped you'll be to help them navigate the ups and downs of transition.

Why Emotions Matter in Transition

Big moves stir up big emotions. One of the greatest gifts you can give your children during this time is the freedom to feel. Excitement, fear, anger, confusion, and sadness are valid, expected, and all welcome.

In I Have to Be Perfect: And Other Parsonage Heresies, Timothy L. Sanford explores the silent expectations often placed on ministry children—expectations to be grateful, happy, and emotionally "together." Many Third-Culture Kids (TCKs) grow up thinking that expressing complicated emotions is wrong or weak. But this belief only buries what needs to be named.

Emotions are not signs of weakness.
They are signals and stories waiting to be shared.

When your family creates space for emotional honesty, you help your children build resilience, courage, and trust. That's what it takes to thrive through transition—not perfection, but presence.

👨‍👩‍👧 Parent Task: Creating a Home Where Feelings Are Welcome

💡 Why it matters:

If children are to process transition well, they need caregivers who create emotionally safe environments. That begins with you. Your attitudes, habits, and personal history with emotion shape how your children experience and express their own.

What to Do:

- **Reflect First**

Ask yourself:
What emotions were accepted in my home growing up?
Were any seen as too much, too weak, or inappropriate?
How might that affect how I respond to my children's emotions now?

- **Model Emotional Openness**

Let your children see you name your emotions without shame:
"I'm feeling sad today about saying goodbye."
"I'm feeling excited but also nervous."
This permits them to do the same.

- **Use Tools That Help Kids Express Themselves**

Introduce simple tools and language to make emotional expression a regular part of family life. Don't wait for a meltdown—build the muscle now while things are calm.

📝 Reflect and Plan

Questions to Consider:

What big feelings are showing up in our family right now?

How does each of my children express (or hide) their emotions during change?

How can I create space for my children to name their feelings without judgment?

What emotions am I experiencing as a parent—and how am I modelling healthy processing?

Write your reflections below:

Child 1:
What feelings are they showing (or not showing)? What helps them feel heard or supported?

Child 2:
What feelings are they showing (or not showing)? What helps them feel heard or supported?

Child 3:
What feelings are they showing (or not showing)? What helps them feel heard or supported?

My reflections on supporting emotions in transition:

👨‍👧‍👦 Family Task: Drawing and Naming Emotions

Help your children express their feelings through creativity and conversation. This works exceptionally well for kids who don't yet have the vocabulary for complex emotions.

Try This Together:

Grab some paper, crayons, or markers. Ask each person to:
- Draw how you feel about the move.
- Show where that feeling is in your body. (e.g., tight chest, butterflies in the stomach)
- Name the feeling with a colour, face, or monster.

You can use these prompts to talk about gently:
- What makes them feel that way
- What they need when that feeling shows up
- How you can help each other as a family

Practical Strategies for Ongoing Emotional Support

Use Feeling Words Regularly

Help your children build a rich emotional vocabulary to express what they're going through.
Try This:
- Use feelings cards at mealtime or bedtime
- Ask: "What colour is your heart today?" or "Which card matches how you feel?"

Helpful Tools:

- Moody Monster Cards (Interwoven)
- The Bear Cards
- Funky Fish Feelings Cards
- Inside Out Emotion Wheel
- The Boy with Big, Big Feelings by Britney Winn Lee
- How Do I Feel? by Rebekah Lipp & Craig Phillips
- Braver, Stronger, Smarter (for girls ages 6–11)

Give Permission to Feel

Sometimes, children worry that sadness, anger, or fear means they're doing something wrong or being ungrateful. Reassure them:
- "It's okay to feel all your feelings. They don't make you bad or wrong—they make you human."
- You don't need to fix everything. Being present, listening, and validating what they say builds trust and emotional safety.

Create Family Check-In Moments

Build rhythms of emotional honesty into your family's week.
Try This:
- Start a "Highs and Lows" tradition. Ask:

"What was the best part of your day?"
"What was the hardest part?"
- Use this as a consistently shared space during car rides, dinner, or bedtime.

Make a "Feelings Are Welcome" Poster

Work together to create a poster that says:
- "All Feelings Are Welcome in Our Family."
- Decorate it with drawings, emoji faces, or emotional monsters. Hang it where everyone can see it.

Companion Activity Ideas

"Today I felt _____ because _____."

"A feeling I don't like to talk about is _____."

"If my feelings were a monster, it would look like…"

WHAT ARE YOU feeling?

 happy
 Embarrassed
 Bored
 Panicked

 excited
 Calm
 Sad
 Scared

 Mad
 confused
 Relaxed
 Tired

 Suprised
 Lonely
 Joyful
 nervous

 Disappointed
 Cheerful
 Angry
 silly

✅ **Key Takeaways for Parents:**

- Emotions are valid and necessary—make space for them.
- Your own emotional awareness models safety and strength.
- Tools like drawings, cards, and routines help kids express what's hard to say.
- Small conversations now build long-term resilience and trust.

Section 5:

Goodbyes & Grief
– Helping Your Family Leave Well

🌐 Overview

This chapter is about more than just logistics or packing lists about creating a safe space for grief, gratitude, and saying goodbye. For Third Culture Kids (TCKs), goodbyes are a natural part of life- they often say goodbye every six months to friends, teachers, favourite routines, languages, houses, pets, and sometimes even parts of their identity.

These goodbyes can leave deep emotional marks, especially if they are not acknowledged. As a parent, you have a wonderful opportunity to help your children navigate these farewells in a healthy way—by honouring what they are saying goodbye to, making room for their feelings, and guiding them into new chapters with understanding and kindness.

Why Grief Is Different for TCKs

TCKs experience a specific kind of layered, ongoing grief. It's not always loud or obvious. Sometimes, it comes out in behaviour, silence, or unexpected places.

Everyday grief experiences for TCKs:
- Frequent goodbyes: They say goodbye often—and not just to people.
- Complex loss: Children may grieve sights, smells, food, playgrounds, pets, sounds, routines, and even language.
- Unspoken grief: They may not know how to explain their sadness—or worry they'll be told to "be thankful" instead.
- Emotional disorientation: Children may feel torn between sadness about leaving and pressure to be excited for what's ahead.

Helping your children name, understand, and express this grief will strengthen their long-term resilience—and deepen their sense of identity and belonging.

The RAFT Model: A Guide to Leaving Well

One of the most effective tools for navigating transition is the RAFT model—an acronym introduced by David C. Pollock and Ruth E. Van Reken in Third Culture Kids: Growing Up Among Worlds. RAFT stands for Reconciliation, Affirmation, Farewell, and Think Destination, and it offers a simple yet powerful framework to guide families through the often-complex process of saying goodbye.

As you explore each part of the RAFT together, consider building a miniature raft out of sticks, string, and leaves. Let this hands-on activity become a symbol of the emotional preparation you're doing as a family. Once built, float it down a creek, pond, or even in a bowl—marking your journey of letting go and moving forward with intention.

Reference: Pollock, D. C., Van Reken, R. E., & Pollock, M. V. (2017). Third Culture Kids: Growing Up Among Worlds (3rd ed.). Nicholas Brealey Publishing.*

R – Reconciliation
- Help your children repair relationships before they leave.
- Ask: "Is there anyone you want to say sorry to?"
- Model forgiveness in your own friendships and work relationships.
- Teach that unfinished conflict often travels with us unless we make peace.

A – Affirmation
- Encourage children to thank the people who've made an impact.
- Write thank-you cards
- Create a small gift
- Record video messages
- Draw a picture for a teacher, house helper, or local friend
- Affirming others reminds children they are part of something meaningful.

F – Farewell
- Say goodbye intentionally—to people, places, pets, routines, and even objects.
- Visit key places one more time
- Say goodbye to your home room by room
- Build farewell events into your schedule
- Saying goodbye doesn't remove sadness, but it honours what mattered.

T – Think Destination
- Look ahead. Explore what's next.
- Look at photos or videos of the new place
- Talk about what may be the same and what may be different
- Let children ask questions and imagine what's ahead
- Holding space for both sadness and curiosity builds emotional flexibility.

👨‍👩‍👧 Parent Task: Reflecting on Grief and Goodbyes

💡 Why it matters:

Every child experiences grief differently. Some will talk about it. Some won't. Some will cry; some will become quieter or more irritable. Your role is to pay attention—to ask, listen, and honour what your children are holding.

What to Do:

Reflect Privately
Take time to consider each of your children:
- What does this child hold dear?
- How do they typically express sadness or worry?
- Is there something they might be grieving that I've missed?

Meet One-on-One
Set aside time with each child. Ask:
- "Is there someone or something you'd like to say goodbye to?"
- "What do you want to bring with you?"
- "What are you wondering about our next home?"

Let your children take ownership of how and what they pack and how they say goodbye.

📝 Reflect and Plan

Questions to Consider:
What kinds of goodbyes are happening in our family right now?

How do I personally approach endings?

How can I help my children grieve in healthy, meaningful ways?

Write your reflections below:

Child 1:
Goodbyes to plan, emotional needs:

Child 2:
Goodbyes to plan, emotional needs:

Child 3:
Goodbyes to plan, emotional needs:

My reflections on leaving:

👨‍👩‍👧 Family Task: Create a Goodbye Plan Together

Leaving well doesn't happen accidentally—it occurs when families make time to remember, reflect, and celebrate.
Steps to Take Together:

📝 Make a Goodbye List
As a family, list:
- People to say goodbye to
- Places to visit one last time
- Routines and rituals to honour
- Favourite meal smells, or sounds to enjoy again

📅 Schedule Farewells
- Build goodbyes into your calendar. Don't leave them for the final day. Think:
- Final playdates or walks
- School visits and thank-yous
- A final family meal of your favourite local foods

🎨 Get Creative
- Record video messages or make a goodbye photo book
- Have kids draw goodbye letters or pictures for friends and neighbours.

📸 Capture Life Through Their Eyes
- Give your children a camera or phone to photograph what they love. Let them create a visual memory book for the plane ride.

🌙 End Each Week with a "Memory Moment"
Ask:
- "What will you miss the most this week?"
- "What are you thankful for today?"
- "What do you want to remember forever?"

Companion Activity Ideas

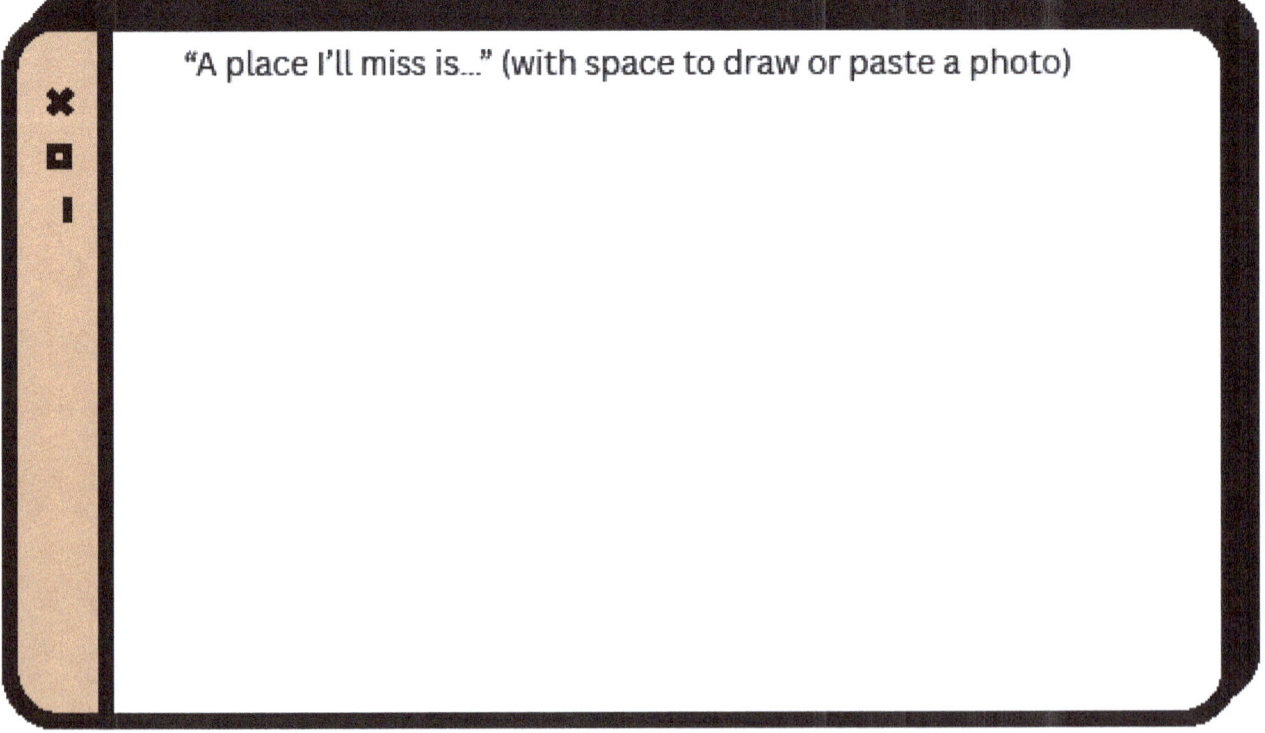

✅ Key Takeaways for Parents:

- TCKs experience frequent and layered grief—naming it helps them heal.
- Goodbyes that are intentional and honouring build emotional resilience.
- The RAFT model gives families a simple, robust roadmap for leaving well.
- Saying goodbye well is not just about closure—it's about carrying memories with grace.

Section 6:

Practical Tips for Moving Overseas and Traveling with Children

Packing, Planning, and Travel Prep for Families

 Overview

The move overseas doesn't start when you land—it begins the moment your family starts preparing to leave. Whether it's the chaos of packing or the long-haul flight with little ones, this section is your go-to guide for navigating the practical side of transition. With thoughtful preparation, your travel experience can become an opportunity for bonding, learning, and building resilience.

Why It Matters

Children are sensitive to uncertainty, and the physical move is full of it—changing environments, disrupted routines, emotional goodbyes, unfamiliar airports, and jet lag. By involving them early, preparing intentionally, and equipping them for what's ahead, you help them feel safe and capable. A smooth transition sets the tone for your first weeks overseas.

 Parents Task

Your role during this transition is part project manager, part emotional anchor. These practical steps are designed to reduce stress, anticipate your family's needs, and create moments of stability and connection. Preparing well— especially with your children in mind—helps smooth the path for what comes next.

Checklist

- Finalise important documents: passports, visas, immunisation records, birth certificates, school records.

- Pack a "First Week Box": essentials you'll need before your shipment arrives (sheets, towels, basic kitchen gear, kids' toys and books, comfort items, snacks).

- Prepare your carry-ons:
    - Spare clothes for everyone
    - Wipes, tissues, sanitiser
    - Entertainment (drawing kits, card games, audiobooks)
    - Special comfort toy or item per child
    - Any required medications

- Teach your child what to expect at the airport: role-play check-in, security, and boarding.

- Research what's difficult to find or expensive in your new country (medications, formulas, feminine hygiene, homeschool supplies, allergy-friendly food, etc.).
- Think about travel day support: snacks, downtime, movement breaks, emotional check-ins.

📝 **Reflect and Plan**

Questions to Consider:
What parts of the move or travel feel most overwhelming right now?

What routines or rhythms could help create stability in this season?

What practical steps can I take to reduce stress and bring a sense of calm?

How can I prepare each of my children to feel included, safe, and confident during the move?

Write your reflections below:

Child 1:
Travel prep needs, emotional support, packing considerations:

Child 2:
Travel prep needs, emotional support, packing considerations:

Child 3:
Travel prep needs, emotional support, packing considerations:

My reflections on preparing to move and travel as a family:

👨‍👩‍👧 Family Task

- Let each child pack a carry-on with travel items.

- Create a visual countdown calendar with moving-related tasks and celebrations.

- Choose a travel mascot (a toy or character) that comes on the journey and gets its photo taken along the way.

- Start a travel journal together—draw or write one page per stop.

📖 Companion Activity Ideas

- Suitcase Sorting Sheet: What goes in the carry-on? What goes in the big suitcase?
- Airport Adventure Map: Draw the journey from home to the gate.
- Emotion Monster Pick: How are you feeling today about the move? Use the cards to talk about it.
- Create Your Travel Ticket: Fill out a pretend boarding pass with your name, destination, and seat.

✅ Key Takeaways for Parents:

- Involving kids in preparation builds confidence and security
- A well-packed carry-on can save the day
- Travel isn't just logistics—it's an emotional and relational milestone
- Small rituals (like a mascot or journal) create continuity across change

Section 7:

Entering In – Preparing Your Children for a Move to a New Country

 Overview

Leaving isn't just about saying goodbye; it's also about arriving with curiosity, courage, and a clear head. Moving to a new country brings a wave of "hellos" that can be both exciting and a bit overwhelming, or anything in between.

Every child will respond in their own way, depending on their age, personality, past experiences, and emotional maturity. Some might jump in with wide-eyed wonder, while others might step back, feeling a little lost or hesitant. Both reactions are completely normal.

It's so important to understand your child and what helps them feel secure. Are they more of an introvert who needs quiet time and space to recharge after meeting new people? Or are they an extrovert who thrives on social activities and group play? Recognising their temperament can help you create routines and environments that nurture their emotional strength and help them feel they belong.

This part of your journey is about preparing for what's ahead- emotionally, practically, and in building relationships.

The Four Stages of Culture Shock

When children move to a new country, they go through cultural shock – the physical and emotional reaction to being in a new environment. Unlike adults, children might not have the words to explain their feelings, but their bodies and behaviour often give them away.

Honeymoon Stage
Everything feels new and fun! Your child might be excited about different foods, clothes, smells, and sounds.

Hard Stage
Reality hits home. Things start to feel too different. Children might get homesick, frustrated or sad as the excitement wears off.

Settling In
Little by little, your child begins to get used to things. They start routines, make friends, and feel more comfortable.

Feeling at Home
With time, your child may start to feel like they belong. They understand how things work and might even enjoy some of the new culture.

Adapted from the original Four Stages of Culture Shock model by Kalervo Oberg (1954).

Signs of Culture Shock in Children

As children adjust to a new culture, their emotions often show up indirectly or unexpectedly. Here are some common signs to watch for:

- Withdrawing and needing alone time. Your child may spend more time in their room, avoid social situations, or seem less interested in interacting with others.
- Emotional ups and downs or outbursts. You might notice increased crying, anger, or sensitivity to small matters.
- Changes in sleep or appetite can indicate emotional stress. Kids may struggle to fall asleep, wake up often, or lose interest in food—or eat more for comfort.
- Physical complaints without clear medical reasons, like stomach aches or headaches, can signal emotional distress.
- Low motivation or school resistance. Children may seem disinterested in learning, hesitant with schoolwork, or overwhelmed by the new system.

These signs don't always indicate serious issues, but they show your child is adjusting and needs extra support, connection, and patience. Keep communication open, establish comforting routines, and allow space for difficult feelings and moments of happiness.

👨‍👩‍👧 Parent Task: Preparing for the New Together

💡 Why it matters:

When you explore a new culture with your child, you build shared excitement, decrease fear of the unknown, and model a posture of curiosity and humility.

What to Do:

Learn Together
Research your destination as a family:
- What is traditional food?
- What language is spoken?
- What is a school like? What do kids wear?
- What will the weather be like?

Start now to build cultural understanding and set realistic expectations.

Practice New Habits
- Learn how to say "hello" and "thank you."
- Try local foods together at home.
- Explore basic language using apps like Duolingo or Drops.
- Watch a cartoon or kids' show in the local language or from a new culture.

✏️ Reflect and Plan

Questions to Consider:
How do I typically react when I'm unsure? What message does that send to my kids?

What parts of this transition are we excited about? Nervous about?

What's one thing I can model this week to prepare for our arrival?

Write your reflections below:
New foods to try together:

Phrases to learn in the new language:

Topics to explore (school, weather, daily life):

Write your reflections below:

Child 1:
What are they most curious, excited, or anxious about? What support will help them adjust to a new environment?

Child 2:
What are they most curious, excited, or anxious about? What support will help them adjust to a new environment?

Child 3:
What are they most curious, excited, or anxious about? What support will help them adjust to a new environment?

My reflections on helping our family prepare to 'enter in':

👨‍👧 Family Task: Make the New Country Come Alive

Help your children visualise and emotionally prepare for where they are going.

Try These Together:

🖼️ Create a Presentation

Let each child help make a fun slideshow or poster about your destination to share with friends or family. Include:
- Photos of landmarks, animals, clothing, food
- A map and flag of the country
- Fun facts about language, sports, or school life

🥮 Try New Foods

Find a recipe or restaurant that features local dishes from your new country. Make it a family-tasting night.

🎙️ Learn Local Phrases

Turn it into a game! Learn how to say:
- Hello
- Goodbye
- Thank you
- My name is…

Use YouTube or language apps together to practice.

📺 Watch a Local Kids' Cartoon or Video

Search for child-friendly content from the new culture. Ask your kids what they notice. What's the same? What's different?

Companion Activity Ideas

"Something I'm looking forward to is

Facts about your new country

Adventure Awaits

✅ **Key Takeaways for Parents:**

- Cultural shock is regular and temporary. Understanding its phases prepares you to respond with empathy.
- Open communication, routines, and cultural learning reduce fear and promote adaptation.
- Curiosity is contagious. When you model openness and flexibility, your children are more likely to follow your lead.
- Preparing early makes children feel like participants in the journey—not just passengers.

Section 8:

Seeing with New Eyes – Helping Your Children Understand Wealth and Poverty in a New Culture

🌍 Overview

Adapting to a new culture involves more than just learning a language or trying different foods; it includes addressing different ways of life and new perspectives on wealth and poverty. As your child immerses in their host culture, they may notice unfair or confusing aspects, like street kids, beggars, gated homes, or stark differences between schools and houses.

While these moments can be overwhelming, they present opportunities for growth. By guiding your children to process these experiences with empathy, you'll shape their worldview and character for years to come.

Why This Matters

Children often see things with a raw honesty. When they notice poverty or inequality, they might ask tough questions:
- "Why don't they have a bed?"
- "Why is that child selling things on the street?"
- "Are we rich now?"

Instead of dodging these moments, engage your child to create opportunities for learning and compassion. Understanding wealth and poverty across cultures helps children develop global awareness and resilience.

👪 Parent Task: Guiding Conversations About Poverty and Privilege

💡 Why it matters:
Your children may now be seen as "rich" in their new culture, which can be disorienting or uncomfortable, especially when compared to how they lived in their home country. Helping them cope with this reality in an empathetic and genuine way will support their cultural adjustment and emotional growth

What to Do:

Initiate Open Discussions
- Talk honestly about how wealth and poverty look in your new context.
- Ask: "What differences have you noticed since arriving?"
- Acknowledge that feeling confused or sad about what they see is okay.

Use Stories and Media
- Choose age-appropriate books or documentaries that explore real-life experiences in your host country.
- Watch a film or read a story together and discuss how it made them feel.

Explore Global Perspectives
- Use tools like Gapminder.org to compare living conditions and economic realities worldwide.
- Discuss how your own family might appear to others and what that means.

📝 Reflect and Plan

Questions to Consider:

How did I first learn about wealth and poverty?

What messages do I want to pass on to my children?

How can we help our kids respond with compassion instead of shame or guilt?

Write your reflections below:

What our kids might observe:

Conversations we want to have as a family:

Ways to model empathy and respect:

👨‍👩‍👧‍👦 Family Task: Exploring Economic Differences Together

Try This Together:

Gapminder Exploration

- Visit www.gapminder.org together as a family.
- Search for your passport country and your new country.
- Compare statistics like income levels, access to education, and health indicators.
- Ask: "What surprised you?" "What do you wonder about?"
- Reflect on what life might be like for a child your age in each country.

Talk About Wealth and Resources

Over dinner or during family devotions, explore:
- "What does it mean to be rich?"
- Why do some people have more than others?"
- "How can we be generous with what we have?"

Share Stories from Both Sides

- Tell stories from your childhood that reflect different experiences with money, community, and generosity.
- Invite grandparents or friends from different countries to share, too.

Helpful Tips for Parents

Normalise the Questions

Children may ask uncomfortable things in public. Don't shame them. Gently guide the conversation later, using their curiosity as a starting point for reflection.

Encourage Empathy Over Pity

Teach your children to see everyone they meet as someone with value and dignity—not a project to be fixed, but a person to be understood.

Create a Safe Place to Talk

Let your children share what confuses or worries them. Validate their feelings:
- "That's a good question."
- "It's okay to feel sad when we see something unfamiliar."
- "I'm still learning too."

Companion Activity Ideas

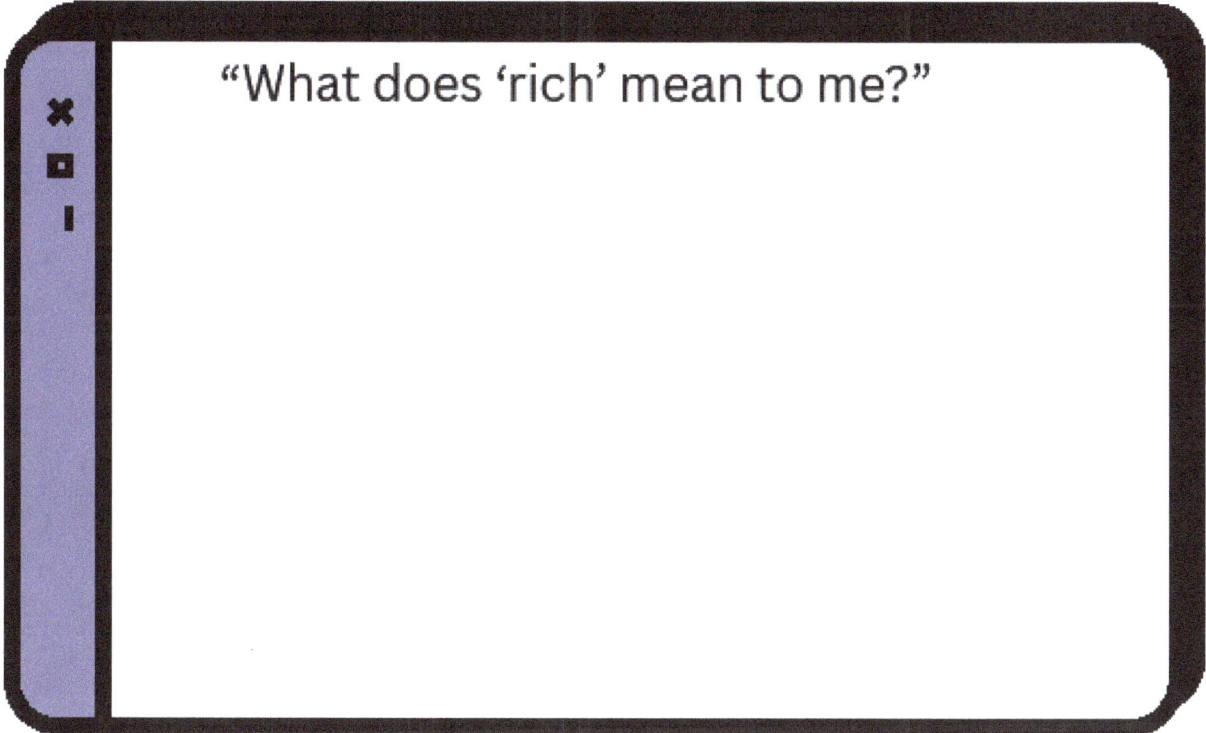

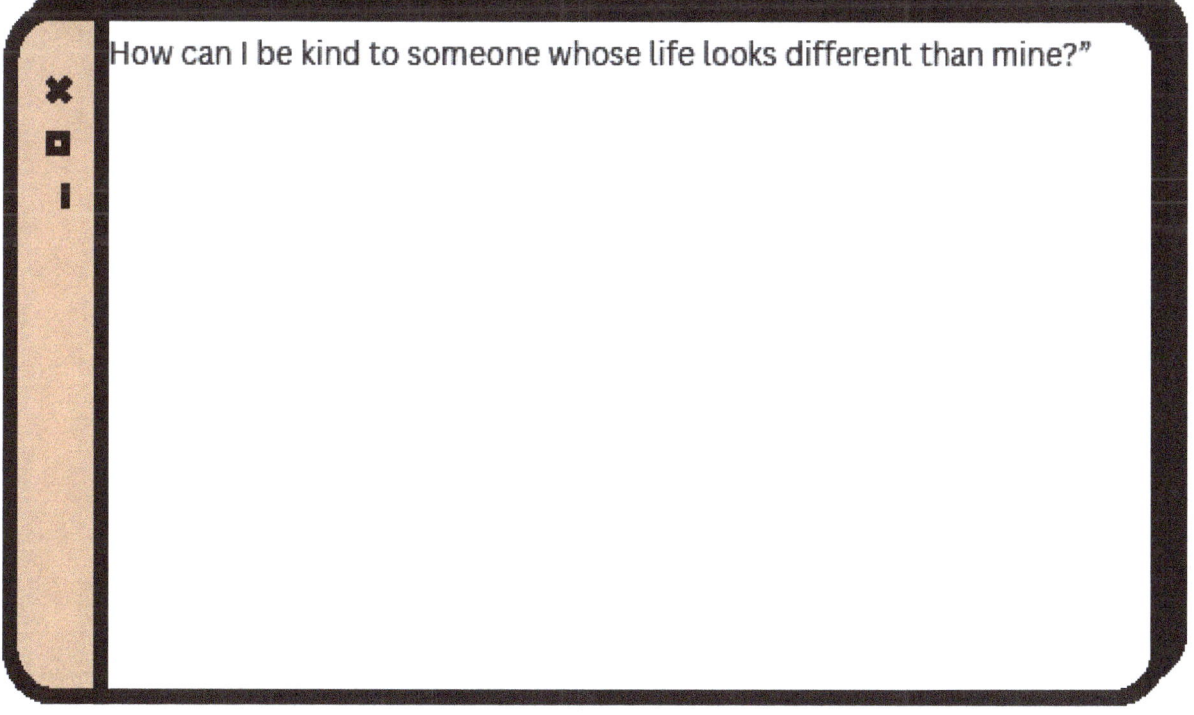

✅ Key Takeaways for Parents:

- Wealth and poverty are interpreted differently in every culture—helping children understand this fosters compassion and global awareness.
- Your family's perceived status may change—talk about it openly and honestly.
- The goal is empathy, not guilt. Guide your children to ask questions, learn deeply, and respond with kindness and respect.
- Simple conversations now build lifelong sensitivity to justice, equity, and generosity.

Section 9:
Important Questions to Ask Along the Way
Understanding Power Distance, Culture, and Family Expectations

🌎 Overview

Cross-cultural life is full of moments that challenge our assumptions—how we relate to authority, make decisions, or express respect. These aren't just surface differences. They're shaped by deep cultural values. This section helps your family reflect on those underlying norms—like power distance—and prepares you to engage your new culture with curiosity, humility, and care.

Why It Matters

Misunderstandings often stem not from bad intentions, but from unspoken expectations. In some cultures, children are expected to speak boldly; in others, silence is a sign of respect. Parents may find themselves confused by school discipline systems or surprised by how independence is (or isn't) encouraged. Helping your children interpret these shifts gives them tools to belong without losing themselves.

 Parents Task

As parents, your job isn't to know all the answers but to create space for observation, questions, and healthy conversation. This task is about becoming a student of your host culture—and helping your kids do the same.

Checklist:

- Learn about your host culture's approach to:
    - Authority and decision-making
    - Teacher/student or adult/child relationships
    - Communication (direct vs indirect)
    - Public behavior and emotional expression
- Talk with locals or teammates about cultural expectations.
- Reflect as a couple/family: What values do we want to hold onto? What are we open to flexing on?
- Model curiosity—when you're confused or surprised, let your children see you ask questions and seek understanding.
- Prepare your children: "Things might be different here, and that's okay. We can learn together."

 **Reflect and Plan**

Questions to Consider:
What parts of the new culture might feel surprising or uncomfortable for our family?

How do we define respect in our home, and how might that differ overseas?

What values do we want to carry with us into this new culture?

How can I help my children process things they don't understand without feeling ashamed or rude?

Write your reflections below:

Child 1:
Cultural awareness needs, questions they may ask:

Child 2:
Cultural awareness needs, questions they may ask:

Child 3:
Cultural awareness needs, questions they may ask:

My reflections on adjusting to new cultural expectations:

👨‍👩‍👧 Family Task

- Create a Culture Comparison Chart: -Fold a page in half—one side for "What We're Used To," one side for "What We're Learning."
  -Talk about rules, greetings, adult/child dynamics, time, and emotions.
- Try Role Play Scenarios: -"What if someone speaks very loudly to you?"
  "What if you're asked to greet an elder differently than usual?"
  -"What if you don't understand why something is a rule?"
-
  Family Check-In: Ask each child once a week, "What's something that felt different to you this week?"

Companion Activities

- Culture Glasses Worksheet: Draw a pair of glasses and write values each lens sees.

- Feeling Monster Card: "What does your monster look like when it doesn't understand the rules?"

- Interview a Local: Ask, "What's one thing kids in this culture are taught about respect?"

✅ Key Takeaways

- Cultural understanding is a skill that takes time
- Permission to ask questions
- You can stay rooted in your values while being open to learning from others
- Respect looks different around the world—learning this builds compassion

Section 10:

Staying Safe – Helping Your Children Feel Secure in a New Culture

🌍 Overview

Moving to a new country means encountering new routines, environments, and social expectations—and with that comes the need for new safety conversations. What feels "normal" or "safe" in one country may look very different in another.
Helping your children build awareness, confidence, and practical safety strategies equips them to navigate their surroundings with wisdom and resilience. When children feel safe, they are more likely to explore, build relationships, and thrive in unfamiliar settings.

Why Safety Conversations Matter

Children are adaptable, but they also need clear guidance. In new environments, everyday activities like crossing the street, greeting a neighbour, or asking for help may look different.

Without proactive conversations, children may become confused, anxious, or vulnerable. When safety rules and boundaries are taught before something happens, children are empowered—not scared.

Key Areas of Safety to Address

Communication

Keep communication open and frequent. Let your children know they can come to you with anything—even if they're unsure or afraid.

Talk through new safety rules specific to the country:
- How do you cross the street safely?
- What do you do if there's an earthquake, power outage, or flood?
- What if someone gets lost in a marketplace?

Cultural Norms

Understanding local customs helps your child navigate social situations safely and respectfully:
- How do people greet each other?
- How are children expected to interact with adults or elders?
- Are there cultural expectations around modesty, meals, or behaviour in public?

Teaching these cultural cues can prevent misunderstandings and foster respectful interactions.

Personal Boundaries

Boundaries may be perceived differently in the host culture—but your child still needs to know:
- They are allowed to say no to unsafe or uncomfortable touch.
- They should respect others' personal space and boundaries, too.
- It's okay to seek help if something feels wrong.

Emergency Preparedness

Ensure your children:
- Know how to contact you or another trusted adult
- Have local emergency numbers written down or saved
- Understand who safe adults are in your new community (e.g., local police, school staff, trusted neighbours)

Safe Places

Show your children:
- Where to go if they feel unsafe (e.g., embassy, friend's house, police station)
- How to get there
- What to say when asking for help

Role-Playing Scenarios

Practice everyday situations through role-play:
- What to do if they get lost
- How to respond if approached by a stranger
- How to handle peer pressure or feeling unsafe at school

These scenarios help build muscle memory and reduce panic in real moments.

Trusting Instincts

Teach your children to trust their gut:
- "If something feels wrong, it's okay to leave—even if you're unsure why."
- Help them know that safety matters more than social politeness or fear of embarrassment.

👨‍👩‍👧 Parent Task: Talking About Body Safety and Consent

💡 Why it matters:

Body safety is foundational in every culture. Your child needs to know they are the boss of their body and that there are clear boundaries no one should cross—no matter where they live.

What to Do:

Have a Body Safety Talk
- Use clear, age-appropriate language to explain:
- Use the correct names for Private body parts
- Safe vs unsafe touch
- The importance of saying no, even to adults
- That it's always okay to tell you—even if someone says to keep it a secret

Teach them The Underwear Rule (PANTS)
Developed by the NSPCC, the PANTS rule helps children understand that their bodies belong to them and gives them tools to speak up if something feels wrong.

P – Privates are private
Your underwear covers the parts of your body that are private. No one should ask to see or touch them. And you shouldn't ask to see or touch someone else's private parts.

A – Always remember your body belongs to you
Your body is yours. No one has the right to make you do anything that makes you uncomfortable. You can say no—even to adults.

N – No means no
You have the right to say no, and it's okay to speak up even if it's to someone you know or love.

T – Talk about secrets that upset you
Some secrets are not safe to keep—especially ones that make you feel worried or uncomfortable. You should always talk to a safe adult.

S – Speak up, someone can help
If you ever feel unsure or unsafe, tell a trusted adult like a parent, teacher, or another grown-up who will listen and help.

This conversation may feel awkward, but it can be lifesaving. Reinforce it regularly.

Based on the PANTS Rule developed by the NSPCC (nspcc.org.uk).

✏️ Reflect and Plan

Questions to Consider:
What are the most significant safety differences between our passport and host country?

Have we talked openly about body safety in a way each child can understand?

What situations might be confusing or risky for our children?

Write your reflections below:
Top three safety rules we want to establish:

Things that may feel new or confusing to our kids:

How we'll reinforce safety over the coming months:

👨‍👩‍👧 Family Task: Create an Emergency Safety Card

Help your children prepare by creating a personalised safety card in their bag, wallet, or school folder.

Include:
- Full name
- Parent names
- Local phone numbers
- Backup contact (e.g., team member, local friend)
- Local emergency number (police/ambulance)
- Home address (written in both English and local language, if possible)

A simple phrase in the local language: "Please help me call my parent."

Decorate the card together and laminate it for durability.

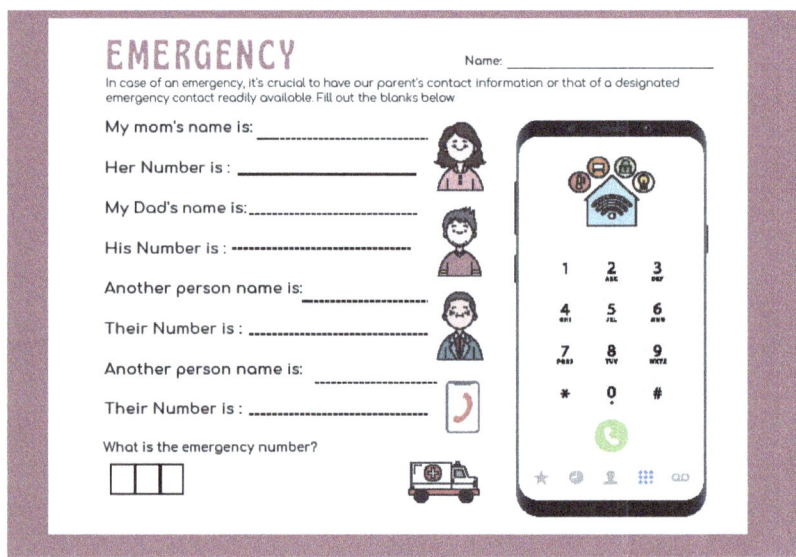

 Companion Activity Ideas

Child Safety Plan Checklist
Review and update regularly (e.g., quarterly or before any major transition)

✓	What I Need to Know	My Notes / Answers
☐	Who are my safe adults?	These are grown-ups I trust and can talk to if I feel worried. (e.g., Mum, Dad
☐	What are my private parts?	I know my private parts are the areas covered by my underwear. No one should touch them, and I don't touch other people's.
☐	What's our family code word?	If someone comes to pick me up and says this word, I know it's safe. Our code word is: _____
☐	What can I do if something feels wrong?	I can say NO, walk away, and tell a safe adult—even if it's someone I know.
☐	What is a safe touch or unsafe touch?	We talked about the difference. I know how to tell the difference and what to do.
☐	Who do I talk to if I have a secret that feels yucky or scary?	I know safe secrets are like birthday surprises, but unsafe secrets should always be shared with someone I trust.
☐	Where will I feel safe in our new home or school?	Some safe places might be: _____
☐	What should I remember when I'm online or using a screen?	I won't talk to strangers online or share photos or my name. I'll always check with a grown-up first.
☐	What should I do in an emergency?	I know how to call for help and who to talk to. My emergency contact is: _____
☐	What makes me feel safe and strong?	I feel safe when: _____ I feel strong when: _____

Adventure Awaits

✅ Key Takeaways for Parents:

- Teaching safety expectations is crucial, but it's essential to adapt to different cultures. Be clear and upfront about it.
- Empower your children with the tools and language they need to speak up for themselves.
- Having open conversations about body safety is vital, even when you're travelling overseas.
- Regular check-ins, role-playing, and honest communication help build trust and confidence from the start.

Section 11:

Navigating Education Overseas- A practical guide for selecting schooling options in a cross-cultural context

Overview

Considering your children's education is one of the most critical aspects of preparing for an international move. While your mission agency may provide initial guidance, it's essential to explore the full range of options and determine what will work best for each child. No solution fits all; your child's personality, learning needs, language abilities, and long-term goals should guide your decisions.

You may have academically driven children, some who thrive socially, and others who benefit from stability and familiar environments. All of these factors should be taken into account as you navigate the diverse schooling systems and options available globally.

Understanding Schooling Around the World

School systems' timing, structure, and curriculum differ significantly between countries. Below is a helpful comparison of key countries where families often come from;

Country	Academic Year	School Structure	Curriculum & Key Features
Australia	Jan – Dec	Kindergarten to Year 12	National Curriculum (ACARA); 4 terms; Southern Hemisphere calendar
New Zealand	Jan – Dec	Year 1 to Year 13	NZ Curriculum; holistic focus; emphasis on Māori culture
USA	Aug/Sept-May/June	Kindergarten to Grade 12	State-regulated; Common Core influences; SAT/ACT standardised testing
Canada	Sept – June	Kindergarten to Grade 12	Provincial systems; inclusive and multicultural; strong academic standards
South Korea	Mar – Feb	6 yrs Primary, 3 Middle, 3 High	National curriculum; high academic rigour; many English-medium international options
Netherlands	Aug – July (varies)	Kindergarten + Primary/Secondary	Canton-based systems; early tracking; multilingual; diverse international schools available

Country	Academic Year	School Structure	Curriculum & Key Features
UK	Sept – July	Reception to Year 13	National Curriculum; IGCSE and A-levels; often 3-term academic year
China	Sept – July	6 years Primary 3 years Junior Secondary ,3 years Senior Secondary	National curriculum; exam-driven; Gaokao university entrance exam; international schools common
Singapore	Jan – Nov	Primary 1–6, Secondary 1–4/5, JC/Poly	MOE-regulated; high standards; bilingual education (English + Mother Tongue); PSLE and A-Levels
India	Apr/June – Mar	Kindergarten to Grade 12	CBSE, ICSE, and State Boards; strong academic focus; English widely used in instruction
Africa (varied)	Varies (often Jan–Nov)	Varies by country	Mix of national, French, British, or IB curriculums; quality varies; access varies by region
Brazil	Feb – Dec	Preschool, Grades 1–9 (Fundamental), Grades 10–12 (Médio)	Portuguese-medium; national curriculum; ENEM exam; public schools vary; strong private and international school options in cities

These variations can impact when and how your children start school and how easily they can integrate into new academic systems or transition back to their passport country.

International Curricula Options

Some international schools or homeschooling programs offer global curricula frameworks. Here are some commonly available ones:
- International Baccalaureate (IB):: Recognised for its high academic standards, **strong focus on critical thinking, and global perspective. Provides the Primary Years Programme (PYP), Middle Years Programme (MYP), and Diploma Programme (DP).
- Cambridge International Examinations (CIE) Offers IGCSE and A-Level programs. It is widely recognised and used in British international schools.
- International Baccalaureate (ib) Program: This program offers a flexible credit-based system, often including IB courses, and prepares students for universities worldwide.
- Australian Curriculum: Follows a structured path with Years, culminating in Year 12, and offers the option of either the HSC or VCE exams.

These curricula can provide continuity during transitions and influence university admission options later in life.
-

Local Schools:

Sending your children to local schools can have both benefits and challenges:

✅ Benefits
- Get the most out of the local culture: your kids can dive right into the local way of life, language, and customs, helping them develop a deeper understanding and appreciation of the host country..
- Boost their language skills: attending local schools can really improve their language proficiency, which will give them a head start in their future education and career.
- Make lasting friendships: your kids can form strong bonds with local students, building a support network and feeling more at home in the community.
- Save some cash: local schools are often more affordable than international schools, which can make a big difference to your budget.

⚠️ Challenges
- Adjusting adapting to a new culture and education system can stress your child.
- Language barriers may hinder communication and comprehension, affecting their schoolwork.
- Feeling like an outsider is challenging, especially as one of few international students.
- The local curriculum and teaching methods may differ significantly, requiring adjustment, including different behaviour management rules.

Social & Emotional Wellbeing
- Support varies: Emotional support services may not be available in all local schools, particularly in rural or under-resourced areas.
- Transition stress: Children might experience anxiety or sadness due to unfamiliar routines, high expectations, or social pressures.
- Parental involvement is key: Strong parent-school communication and emotional check-ins at home can help children feel secure and supported.
- Building resilience: Over time, many children gain confidence, flexibility, and cross-cultural empathy—important lifelong traits.

International School:

Sending your children to international schools comes with its own set of benefits and challenges:

✅ Benefits
- Stable curriculum: International schools offer established curricula (e.g., IB, American, British), ensuring a consistent educational experience for frequently relocating families
- Multicultural Environment: Children interact with diverse peers, fostering global awareness.
- Language Proficiency: Many schools provide programs in English or other major languages, enhancing language skills.
- Support Systems: They have resources for students who transition often.
- Global Network: Attending an international school helps children build a global network of friends and contacts for future value.

⚠️ Challenges
- Cost: International schools can be pricey, which might not be within reach for all families.
- Cultural Bubble: They might end up in a cultural bubble, cut off from the local culture and community.
- Limited Local Interaction: Chances to fully integrate and connect with the local population may be limited.
- High Turnover: These schools often have high staff and student turnover rates, which can be tough for forming lasting relationships.
- Academic Pressure: Academic standards in some international schools can be tough and stressful for students.

Social & Emotional Wellbeing

- Transition-aware environments: Many international schools have systems in place to support Third Culture Kids (TCKs) and globally mobile students, including peer mentoring and orientation programs.
- Emotional support services: School counsellors and pastoral care teams are often available, especially in larger schools.
- Identity and belonging: While students often find solidarity among fellow TCKs, they may still struggle with questions of identity, frequent goodbyes, and loss.
- Parental role: Regular emotional check-ins and involvement in school life can help children manage the ups and downs of international education.

Boarding School

Boarding schools may suit families with children who frequently relocate or live in remote areas. However, sending your child to boarding school is a significant decision that requires careful consideration of their age, personality, and emotional maturity.

Suitable for: Older kids (usually 12+) who are mature and independent adaptable.

✅ Benefits

- Stable Environment: Boarding schools offer a stable and consistent setting, which can be really important for kids who move around a lot.
- High Academic Standards: Many boarding schools have top-notch academic programs, giving students a solid educational base.
- Diverse Community: Boarding schools often have students from all sorts of backgrounds, promoting cultural exchange and global understanding.
- Independence: Going to boarding school can help them develop independence, self-discipline, and life skills.
- Extracurricular Opportunities: Boarding schools usually have heaps of extracurricular activities, from sports to arts, letting students explore and develop their interests.

⚠️ Challenges

- Being Apart from Family: Being away from family for long periods can be tough on some kids, making them feel homesick, abandoned and isolated.
- Cultural Clash: They might feel disconnected from their host and family cultures, which can affect their sense of identity and belonging.
- Pressure and Stress: The academic and social pressures of boarding school can be really intense, causing stress and anxiety.
- High Costs: Boarding schools can be pricey, which might not be affordable for all families.
- Getting Used to the New Environment: Initially, adjusting to boarding school life can be tricky, requiring a bit of time to get used to.

Social & Emotional Wellbeing

- Emotional support varies: Many boarding schools offer pastoral care, counselling, and structured support—but the quality and approach can differ.
- Identity and belonging: Students may struggle with their sense of identity and home, especially if culturally isolated.
- Resilience and coping: Some students flourish with increased independence, while others may need additional emotional support.
- Family connection matters: Regular communication, scheduled visits, and open emotional dialogue help children feel secure and supported from a distance.

Homeschooling

For globally mobile families, homeschooling is a growing choice. It offers flexibility, continuity, and the flexibility to tailor learning to a child's needs—especially useful during regular moves or when local school options are limited.

Choosing a Curriculum

There's no one-size-fits-all approach to homeschooling—families can choose from a broad range of international curricula based on their long-term goals, home country requirements, or the child's learning style.
Here are some commonly used options:

- United Kingdom: follows the National Curriculum for England. Many families use programs like Cambridge International (IGCSE and A-Levels) or Oxford Home Schooling.
- United States: offers a diverse range of homeschooling programs and online schools. Popular curricula include Abeka, Sonlight, and Time4Learning. Families often follow state-specific guidelines to meet future accreditation needs.
- Australia: The Australian Curriculum is a national framework, which each state adapts (e.g., NSW, Victoria). NSW and Queensland syllabi are commonly used abroad and in international schools.
- Canada: Provinces regulate education, and families often register with a provincial board. Programs like North Star Academy or Virtual High School are popular.
- International Baccalaureate (IB): While not commonly used in full at home, some families supplement with IB-aligned resources to prepare for re-entry into IB schools.
- Faith-Based or Unschooling Approaches: Many families blend curriculum options or choose alternative models like Charlotte Mason, Montessori, or unschooling based on family values or child-led learning.

Tip: Check if your passport country requires registration or assessment to maintain educational compliance.

✅ Benefits

- Customised Learning: Homeschooling lets kids learn at their own pace, with an education tailored to their individual needs and interests.
- Flexibility: Families can create a schedule that fits around travel, family time, and other commitments.
- Stable Environment: Homeschooling provides a steady learning environment, which can be reassuring for kids who are used to moving around a lot.
- Family Bonding: This option gives families more time to bond and allows parents to be closely involved in their child's education.
- Protection from Bullying: Reduces exposure to bullying and peer pressure, creating a safer learning space.

⚠️ Challenges

Social Interaction: Not having regular chances to interact with peers can impact the development of social skills.
- Access to Resources: Students might not have access to specialist educational resources, extracurricular activities, and facilities that traditional schools offer.

- Parental Commitment: It takes a lot of time, effort, and dedication from parents to manage the curriculum and teach effectively.
- Standardisation: Making sure the education meets academic standards and requirements can be tough.
- Limited Extracurriculars: There are fewer opportunities for extracurricular activities like sports, music, and art, which are often easily available in schools.

Social & Emotional Wellbeing

- Isolation risks: Without regular peer contact, children may feel lonely or disconnected if not intentionally supported through community groups or co-ops.
- Tailored emotional support: Homeschooling allows for more attentive, responsive care if a child is struggling emotionally.
- Flexible transitions: Easier to adapt learning plans around emotional ups and downs caused by relocation, loss, or adjustment.
- Intentional community building: Families may need to proactively create social opportunities through local clubs, expat networks, church groups, or online classes
- Identity and confidence: Children often develop a strong sense of self and values through personalised learning, though they may need additional support during major transitions or re-entry to formal schooling.

Online Schooling

Online schooling is a formal education delivered through a digital platform, usually by an accredited school or institution. It differs from traditional homeschooling in that certified teachers provide instruction, mark assignments, and often offer live classes. Students follow a set timetable and curriculum, making it ideal for families looking for consistency, accountability, or pathways to recognised qualifications like IGCSEs, A-Levels, or a U.S. high school diploma.

Some popular international online schools include:
- Wolsey Hall Oxford (UK-based)
- Laurel Springs School (USA)
- Australian Christian College Online (Australia)
- International Connections Academy (Global)

This option can benefit TCKs who need a consistent curriculum across countries or are preparing for university entrance.

✅ Benefits

- Flexibility: Online schooling offers flexible schedules, making it easier to manage travel and family commitments.
- Continuity: It provides a consistent education experience, even when families move around a lot.
- Customised Learning: Students can access courses that match their interests and needs, often with advanced or specialised options.
- Access to Resources: They get access to a wide range of learning resources and materials that might not be available locally.
- Parental Involvement: Parents can be more involved in their child's education, helping to track progress and provide support.

⚠️ Challenges

- Social Interaction: Having limited chances to meet with peers face-to-face can affect the development of social skills.
- Technical Issues: Students need reliable internet access and technology, which can be tricky in some areas.
- Self-motivation: They must be self-disciplined and motivated to stay on top of their studies.
- Time Management: Juggling online school with other activities and responsibilities can be tough for students and parents.
- Limited Extracurriculars: Online schooling may offer fewer chances for extracurricular activities like sports, arts, and social clubs.

Social & Emotional Wellbeing

Risk of isolation: Without daily peer interaction, students may feel disconnected or lonely, especially in remote or isolated locations

Supportive environment at home: Success in online schooling often depends on a supportive home setup and emotional encouragement

Flexible emotional pacing: Students can take breaks or adjust workloads to manage stress and transitions

Online community options: Some programs offer virtual clubs, discussion forums, or group projects to support peer connection—but the quality varies

👪 Parent Task: Making Thoughtful Educational Decisions

Choosing the right educational path for your child overseas isn't just about logistics—it's about aligning your family's mission, your children's developmental needs, and long-term goals. Use the tasks below to guide your thinking and planning process.

Discover Your Family's Purpose and Educational Goals
- How do our choices about education align with our values and sense of purpose?
- What does thriving mean to us as a family, and what does it look like for each of our kids?

Map the Long-Term Journey
- Will this option enable a seamless transition back into our home country's education system?
- Could this impact future exams, qualifications, or university applications?

Know Your Timeline
- How long do we expect to be in this country?
- Will our choice hold up if we leave early or stay longer?

Prepare for Transitions
- What academic documentation (portfolios, transcripts, progress reports) will we need?
- Who will be responsible for tracking records if we choose a non-traditional path?

Plan Around Home Assignment
- Does this school calendar fit with our furlough or home assignment plans?
- How might frequent moves affect friendships and academic progression?

Identify Non-Negotiables
- Are there any fixed factors shaping our decision (e.g., finances, language of instruction, theological values, safety concerns)?

Assess Special Educational Needs
- Does our child need additional learning or emotional support?
- Can the school or system accommodate these needs effectively?

Check Compatibility with Passport Country
- Will this curriculum prepare our child for reintegration?
- Are we setting them up well for both academic and social transition?

Learn from Others
- Ask teammates or other families: What worked for you? What would you do differently?

Invite Your Child Into the Conversation
- What excites or worries them?
- What are their hopes, preferences, or fears?
- Let their voice be part of the process, especially as they grow older.

📝 Reflect & Plan

Our top 3 priorities for education as a family are:
1.

2.

3.

What we've learned from other families:

Questions we still need to answer:

Each child's input (likes, needs, worries):
Child 1:

Child 2:

Child 3:

Steps we'll take next:
Research:

Meetings:

Applications:

Conversations with children:

 **Family Task**

Research Possible Schools Together

As a family, explore the websites or virtual tours of schools or educational options. Discuss:
- Curriculum and subjects offered
- Daily routines and school culture
- Languages used
- Uniforms and expectations
- Extracurricular opportunities
- Faith alignment (if relevant)

This helps build familiarity and reduces anxiety by making the unknown feel more known.

Companion Activity Ideas

> "What kind of school would I like?"

> "What makes me nervous?""

Adventure Awaits

✅ **Key Takeaways for Parents:**

- Education decisions should consider personality, needs, and long-term goals
- Be flexible: what works in one season may shift
- Ask for help. Talk to others. Involve your kids.
- Track progress and prepare for transitions
- Honour both your child's growth and your family's calling

Section 12:

Additional Needs and Neurodiversity

Supporting Your Child's Unique Needs When Preparing to Move Overseas

 Overview

Children with additional needs—including those who are neurodivergent or have ongoing medical conditions—may face unique challenges when transitioning to a new country. Planning ahead can ensure their emotional, educational, and physical needs are understood and supported, both during the move and once you've arrived.

Why It Matters

Transitions can be especially stressful for children who thrive on structure, routine, and familiarity. Moving overseas often brings new languages, different healthcare systems, unfamiliar schools, and sensory overload. Without preparation, this can lead to distress, regression, or increased anxiety. Proactive planning helps your child feel safe, included, and empowered—laying the foundation for a smoother, more supported transition.

👨‍👧 Parent Task

- Book any necessary medical or developmental assessments before departure, including updated reports and letters for schools or healthcare providers.
- Research the availability of specialist support and medications in your new country.
- Speak with your sending agency or field team about realistic accommodations in-country.
- Pack a "transition toolkit": calming aids, medical documents, education plans, and comfort items.

Create a summary profile of your child's needs, strengths, and strategies that work well.

📝 Reflect & Plan:

This page is for parents to step back and consider what supports their child will need during the move—and how to advocate for them intentionally and confidently.

Reflection Questions for Parents
What are the unique strengths and challenges our child brings to this transition?

What supports or routines help our child feel calm, focused, or regulated?

Have we gathered updated documentation (diagnoses, IEPs, prescriptions, letters from doctors or therapists)?
☐ Yes ☐ In Progress ☐ Not Yet Started

What supports or therapies will we likely need in our new country?

What might be different or unavailable where we're going?

Planning Checklist

- Book assessments or appointments before departure
- Request school reports and letters from specialists
- Research medication access and bring enough for several months
- Gather all medical and support documentation in a travel folder
- Reach out to the team in your new country about learning or medical needs
- Prepare a support profile for schools or caregivers
- Build a sensory/travel comfort kit

One Sentence Intentions
Before you finish this section write one sentence to guide your family's approach:

"Our priority is to…"

"We will advocate for our child by…"

👨‍👩‍👧 Family Task

- Talk together about what helps each family member feel calm and supported.
- Explore a travel or transition plan as a family—make a visual schedule or story about what to expect.
- Create a "My Needs & Strengths" page for your child's Companion Journal (e.g. I feel calm when…, I don't like…, I love…, I need help with…).
- Practice travel scenarios (airport, loud noises, waiting in line) through play or storytelling.

Celebrate what makes each family member unique—draw, write, or share stories about your "superpowers."

📔 **Companion Journal Activity:**

My Strengths, My Needs, and My Support Plan

This activity helps your child (and you!) express who they are, what helps them feel safe, and how to prepare for what's ahead.

🧠 All About Me
(For your child to draw or write, or for parents to help fill in depending on age)

I feel calm when: _____

I get overwhelmed when: _____

Things that help me feel better: _____

My favorite comfort items: _____

Something I want my new teacher/helper/friend to know about me is:

💼 Packing List for My Unique Needs
Draw or list the items that help you feel safe, calm, and confident.
(Sensory tools, medications, routines, music, snacks, favorite shirt, etc.)

📦 _____
📦 _____
📦 _____

🎞️ My Travel Plan
What might be hard about the trip? What can we do to make it easier?

What might be tricky?
What can we do to help?

Loud airport noises   _____
Waiting in line   _____
Long travel days   _____

Adventure Awaits

116

✅ Key Takeaways

- Plan early: Medical and educational systems vary—don't assume availability or compatibility.
- Communicate clearly: Provide written profiles and documentation for new caregivers or teachers.
- Travel wisely: Prepare for overstimulation, medical needs, or delays with proactive strategies.
- Empower your child: Help them understand and express their needs in age-appropriate ways.

You are not alone: Reach out to global or local networks of support for families with additional needs.

Section 13:

Belonging in Transit: Helping Your Child Define Home

🌎 Overview

"You will never be completely at home again because part of your heart will always be elsewhere." – Miriam Adeney

One of the most common—and complicated—questions Third Culture Kids (TCKs) face is:

"Where is home?"

This question isn't just geographical—it's deeply personal. It can trigger pride, longing, confusion, and grief, all at once. For globally mobile children, home may be where they were born, where their passport says they belong, where their friends live, or where they left their favourite swing set.

Some TCKs will describe home as:
- "The apartment in Hanoi where we had dinner on the floor."
- "The compound where I rode bikes with my neighbours."
- "That guesthouse we stayed in every time we visited the capital."

Others might say:
- "I'm not sure."
- "Nowhere."
- "Wherever we go next."

All of these are valid.

As parents, we often want to offer our children solid answers and clear roots. But the TCK experience invites us into a more layered understanding. Home is not always a fixed destination—it's an evolving concept shaped by places, people, emotions, and belonging.

This section will guide you in:
- Exploring your family's personal story of home
- Equipping yourself for emotionally complex conversations
- Using creative tools to help your child name and hold their own understanding of home

👨‍👩‍👧 Parent Tasks

Reflect on Your Own Experience of Home

- What places have shaped your own sense of identity?
- How have your definitions of home changed over time?
- What unresolved feelings might influence how you speak with your child?

Trace Your Child's Story Through Place

- Write down three physical places that have shaped your child's life:
- What did they gain or lose in each place?
- What values or routines did you carry forward—or leave behind?

Practice Language for Conversations

Prepare to support your child's emotions using phrases like:
- "It's okay to feel torn between places."
- "You don't have to pick just one home."
- "We're learning what home means together."

Prepare to Validate Complex Emotions

When your child expresses guilt for loving one place more than another or feeling "homeless," respond with empathy. Their feelings are valid—even when they don't match your own.

📝 Reflect & Plan

Anticipate the Conversations
Use quiet moments—packing, bedtime, travel—to open conversations:
"What will you miss most?"

"What might help this new place feel like home?"

"What could we bring with us that reminds us of here?"

Name the Layers of Home
Introduce helpful vocabulary:
Passport Country – where they hold citizenship
Host Country – where they will be living
Heart Home – a place they felt deeply connected

Normalize "I Don't Know"
Let children know it's okay not to have a clear answer to "Where is home?"
Offer flexible language like:
"Right now, I feel most at home in…"

"I think I have pieces of home in a few places."

 Family Tasks

Home Map" Activity
- Create a visual map of everywhere your family has lived or visited. Include:
Flags, drawings, or photos
- Favourite foods and memories
- What made each place feel like home—or not

"People Who Feel Like Home" Collage
- List or collage people who anchor your family. These could include:
  Friends, extended family, mentors, teammates
- Talk about what makes these people feel like "home"
- Write or pray for them together

"Home in a Box" Activity
Give each person a small box (or draw one) and ask:
- "If you could carry pieces of home with you, what would you put inside?"
Ideas:
A food wrapper
A photo or keepsake
A song or smell
A small toy or favorite word

"Finish the Sentence" Prompts
Use at mealtimes or car rides:
- "Home is where _____."
- "I feel at home when _____."
- "One thing I wish I could take with me is _____."

Build Your Ideal Home
Use drawings, LEGO, or crafts to imagine your dream home.
Ask:
- What makes it feel safe?
- Who's there?
- What smells, sounds, or routines are present?

Companion Activity Ideas

> Draw my three heart homes

✅ Key Takeaways for Parents

- Home is not just a place—for TCKs, it's often a combination of people, places, and feelings.
- Your child may not have a single definition of home. That's okay.
- Let them carry multiple homes. Help them name and honour each one.
- Give language to the complexity:
    "You don't have to choose just one home."
    "It's okay to feel at home in many places—or nowhere for a little while."

Section 10:

Routines & Rhythms – Creating a Sense of Stability

 ## Overview

For Families Preparing to Move Cross-Culturally for the First Time

When everything else is about to change, routines can be one of your most powerful tools for creating stability. As your family prepares to move cross-culturally, establishing consistent rhythms and predictable touch-points provides a sense of normalcy that helps children feel safe, grounded, and connected—before and after the move.

Why Routines Matter During Cross-Cultural Transition
Routines are more than time management—they're emotional anchors. For children facing new languages, foods, schools, and relationships, routines can:
- Create predictability amidst uncertainty
- Help regulate emotions and reduce anxiety
- Reinforce belonging and identity
- Support healthy habits (e.g., sleep, meals, downtime)
- Strengthen family communication and togetherness.
-

Many Third Culture Kids (TCKs) move through constantly shifting environments. Establishing family rhythms early provides a portable sense of home

What Makes a Good Pre-Move Routine?
- Consistency – Aim for regular wake-up, mealtime, and bedtime routines that can remain stable throughout the move.
- Flexibility – Create rhythms that can adapt to jet lag, culture shock, or new schedules without losing core structure.
- Inclusion – Involve your children in building routines so they feel heard and empowered.
- Relational Touch-points – Prioritise simple daily connections like bedtime stories, morning check-ins, or family prayer.

**Parent Task:**

- Reflect on what rhythms are currently working in your home.
- Identify stress points or chaotic times that might need extra structure.
- Choose 1–2 core daily rituals to implement now—something that could be continued in your new location (e.g., evening reflections, Sunday pancakes).
- Display your routine visually (e.g., whiteboard, printed chart, fridge calendar) so it's easy for everyone to follow and adapt together.

📝 Reflect & Plan

As you prepare to move, routines can help your children feel safe and grounded. Take time to reflect on what works and plan simple rhythms to carry with you.

Reflect

What routines already help our family feel calm and connected?

What small rituals could we introduce now to prepare for the move?

Which routines (like bedtime prayers or Friday dinners) do we want to protect in our new setting?

Plan
- Morning Start: Choose a calming way to begin each day (e.g., shared breakfast or prayer).
- Evening Wind-Down: Keep bedtime routines simple and portable (e.g., story, reflection, prayer).
- Mealtime Anchors: Pick 2–3 meals each week to enjoy together, wherever you are.
- Weekly Rhythm: Include time for learning, rest, creativity, fun, and faith.
- Visual Tools: Use a child-friendly "My Week" chart to help everyone know what to expect.

 **Family Task:**

Create a "My Week" Chart
- Help your children prepare for upcoming changes by creating a visual weekly plan they can interact with.
- Give each child a blank weekly chart to colour or personalise.
- Include broad blocks like "wake-up," "meals," "activities," "quiet time," and "bedtime."
- Use stickers, drawings, or icons to make it fun and age-appropriate.
- Talk about which parts of the routine might stay the same and which may change in your new country.

Display it in a shared family space to create stability and ownership.

📖 Companion Activities

Routine Wheel – Create a paper wheel with segments for different parts of the day (meals, rest, play, learning). Use it to talk about your daily rhythm and what might carry over to your new home.

Clock Matching Game – For younger kids, match pictures of daily activities with clock times to help them understand time and transitions.

Wind-Down Jar – Fill a jar with calming activities your child can choose from before bed (reading, drawing, music, prayer). Helps carry bedtime comfort across cultures.

Meal Planner Together – Let your children help choose meals each week, including familiar comfort foods they love. Continue this after moving to support routine and cultural integration.

✅ Key Takeaways for Parents

- Routines offer emotional safety when everything else is new.
- Even simple rituals—like storytime or shared meals—can create powerful moments of connection.
- Involve your children in building and owning your family rhythms.
- Visual tools and consistent habits increase stability and ease culture adjustment.
- Flexibility within a predictable rhythm helps your family thrive through change.

Section 11:

Language & Communication – Building Bridges Before the Move

🌐 Overview

Language is more than just words – it's about connection, belonging, and understanding. As your family gets ready to move to a new culture, your kids will learn to adapt to new foods, routines, sights, and ways of communicating.

For some, this might mean learning an entirely new language. For others, it may involve getting used to unfamiliar accents, slang, or the cultural meanings behind words. Even speaking the same language in your new country may sound different and feel different.

Helping your kids prepare to communicate across languages and cultures is a crucial part of their transition. It will help ease their anxiety, build their confidence, and maintain relationships with those they're leaving behind.

Why This Matters

Cultural Adaptation
Language is the gateway to connection. It helps children make friends, understand local norms, and feel more at home in their new environment.

Preserving Identity
Keeping a home or heart language alive supports your child's identity and connection to extended family or passport culture.

Emotional Expression
Being able to express feelings in a familiar language helps children process the emotions of leaving, arriving, and adjusting.

Staying Connected
Conversations with loved ones back home require intentional choices—especially when time zones, technology, and languages create barriers.

Common Communication Challenges for First-Time TCKs
- Worry about learning a new or unfamiliar language
- Losing fluency in their first language due to disuse
- Feeling embarrassed or misunderstood
- Code-switching between languages or dialects
- Difficulty staying in touch with far-away friends or relatives

 **Parent Task:**

Language Reflection & Preparation
Before the move, take time to reflect on your family's language values and goals:
- What language(s) do we currently speak at home?
- Are there any languages we hope to preserve or build on in our new setting?
- How do we respond when our children struggle with words or express frustration around communication?
- How can we model curiosity, grace, and patience around language learning?
- Are there relationships (e.g., with grandparents) that require intentional support through language?

📝 Reflect & Plan:

As you prepare for your cross-cultural move, take a few moments to reflect and lay simple plans to support your family's multilingual journey.

Reflect
What languages or phrases feel part of our family identity?

How might each child respond to a new language—what support might they need?

What language routines or traditions do we want to preserve (e.g., bedtime stories, calls with grandparents)?

Plan
- Listen Together: Add songs or stories in the host language to your weekly rhythm.
- Pack Smart: Bring books or apps in both home and host languages.
- Record & Connect: Let children record greetings for loved ones before leaving.
- Learn as a Team: Choose 5–10 key phrases to learn together as a family.
- Stay in Touch: Plan how to maintain contact with friends and family—calls, letters, or shared photo albums.

 **Family Tasks**

Language Exploration Chart
Create a simple 3-column chart as a family:
- Words We Use at Home
- Words We're Excited to Learn
- Words We Miss from Other Places

Invite your children to draw, decorate, or add photos and stickers to make it meaningful and fun.

Staying-in-Touch Toolkit
Plan how you'll maintain connections with people you love after the move:
- Choose a weekly time for video calls or voice messages
- Practice sending drawings, letters, or short emails
- Set up a shared photo album with captions in your home language and the new one

Companion Activities

Music & Media Swap
Explore both comfort and curiosity by:
- Listening to songs in your host country's language
- Watching cartoons or reading simple books in both languages
- Keeping a few favorite shows or bedtime stories in your home language

Family Phrase Game
Turn language learning into fun by:
- Picking 5-10 essential words or phrases to learn together
- Using flashcards, drawing games, or a "word of the day" board

✅ Key Takeaways for Parents
- Language is a powerful bridge—help your child build it from both sides.
- Start the conversation about communication challenges early and often.
- Celebrate your family's multilingual journey, even when it's messy.
- Simple tools and routines can help your child stay connected across cultures and distances.

Section 16:

Faith & Spiritual Formation in Transition- Guiding Your Children Spiritually Through Change

 Overview

Transition often stirs up big questions—not just about where we are going, but who we are, what matters, and where God is in the change. For children, moving to a new country may shake routines that previously gave them spiritual grounding: familiar Sunday school teachers, family devotions, church friends, or youth group mentors.

Yet, this season also presents a powerful opportunity: to help your children discover that God is present not just in places but in every part of their story.

Why This Matters

Spiritual Resilience: Faith can become a source of strength, identity, and hope through transition

Identity Formation: Children are asking, "Who am I?" and "Where do I belong?"—Faith helps anchor their answers

Spiritual Curiosity: New cultures can broaden your children's view of God and the global church

Consistency & Connection: Familiar spiritual practices help children feel grounded in an unfamiliar environment

👪 Parent Tasks: Preparing for Spiritual Transition

Choose Your Anchor Practices

Identify two or three spiritual habits you want to carry into your new season. These might include:
- Evening prayer as a family
- Weekly gratitude journaling
- Worship music during daily routines

Share Your Own Journey of Faith in Transition

Talk with your children about how you're trusting God during this move. Be honest about your hopes, questions, and the ways you see God at work—even when things feel uncertain.

Create Space for Spiritual Questions

Commit to listening without judgment when your children express doubts or fears. Practice responses like:
- "That's a great question."
- "I wonder about that too sometimes."
- "Let's ask God about that together."

Prepare Spiritually Together
Before the move, set aside one or two moments each week for spiritual preparation:
- Read a Bible story or passage that speaks to change, courage, or trust
- Pray specifically for the journey ahead
- Create a "God is With Us" list or poster of ways you've seen His faithfulness in the past

📝 Reflect & Plan: Nurturing Faith in Transition

Moving cross-culturally is not just a physical journey—it's a spiritual one. Take time to reflect and prepare your family's faith life for this next season.

Reflect
What faith practices help anchor us right now?

How are we modelling trust in God during this transition?

Are we creating space for our children's spiritual questions and emotions?

Plan
- Choose 2–3 simple spiritual rhythms to take with you (e.g., prayer, worship, journaling).
- Pack a small "faith kit" with items that help your children feel spiritually grounded.
- Stay open to how faith may grow in new and unexpected ways in your next culture.

 **Family Tasks:**

Growing Faith Together

Pack Your Portable Faith
Talk together about which spiritual practices your family wants to bring with you. These might include:
- Bedtime prayers or worship playlists
- Gratitude journals or memory verses
- Devotional books or illustrated Bibles

Explore Faith Communities
After arriving, visit churches or small groups as a family. Let your children share what feels familiar or different. Include them in choosing a place where you can all grow spiritually.

"God in the Journey" Journal
Invite your children to create a simple journal where they can draw or write:
- Prayers
- Questions about God
- Thankful moments
- Times they felt God's presence

Companion Activity

My Faith on the Move

Start a "God in the Journey" Journal
Use your journal to draw or write about:
- Things that remind you God is with you
- Prayers or questions you have
- Moments you felt peace, wonder, or joy

Faith Milestones Page
Make a page for special faith memories like:
- A time you felt close to God
- A prayer that was answered
- A Bible verse or song that means something to you

My Faith Playlist
List or draw your favourite worship songs or verses.
You can listen to them during packing, flying, or when you feel homesick.

My Prayer List
Write or draw people you want to pray for in this season—family, friends, people you're leaving, or meeting soon.

✅ Key Takeaways
- Faith isn't left behind—it travels with your family
- Your children may experience God in new ways through new cultures.
- Give space for both certainty and doubt, routine and discovery.
- Keep spiritual conversations open, accessible, and relevant to their stage of life.

Section 17:

Debriefing and Planning for Home Assignments

 Overview

Heading back to your passport country for a home assignment isn't just a break—it's a crucial part of your family's global adventure. For kids, it can be a thrilling, weird, or even nerve-wracking experience. Whether you're away for three months or a whole year, how you prepare and tackle this time together counts.
Creating space to reflect on the past and prepare for what's next, you help your children make sense of their experiences and feel more secure in the transitions ahead.

Why This Matters

Home assignment is not simply a break from overseas life. For children, returning "home" can be just as disorienting as moving abroad. Children may carry unresolved emotions, reverse culture shock, or confusion into their next season without time to debrief and intentional planning.

Debriefing allows your child to be seen, heard, and understood. Planning reduces uncertainty and gives the whole family a sense of rhythm and purpose.

What Is a Home Assignment?

A home assignment (or furlough or re-entry) is a season spent in your passport country, usually between 3 to 12 months. Its purpose is to:
- Reconnect with supporters
- Receive rest and care
- Access to education and healthcare
- Spend time with extended family
-

For your children, it may feel like a return to a place that is "supposed to be home" but may not feel that way anymore.

Everyday experiences for TCKs during home assignment:
- Reverse culture shock
- Emotional "whiplash" from changes in structure, friends, or environment
- Excitement and anxiety about seeing family
- Feeling misunderstood or bored

What Is Debriefing?

Debriefing is the intentional act of helping your child reflect on their life overseas. It gives them tools to:
- Name emotions, they might not know how to express
- Celebrate joyful memories and acknowledge what was hard
- Understand their personal growth
- Prepare emotionally for what's ahead

Without debriefing, children may internalise confusion, grief, or cultural tension. With it, they begin to integrate their experience into their identity.

👨‍👩‍👧 Parent Task:

Preparing Your Family for Re-entry

- Reflect on your own journey: What joys and griefs are you carrying into this new season?
- Model reflection and gratitude in front of your children.

Start preparing for home assignment 3–6 months in advance. Think about:
- Will your child attend school ? If on extended home assignment
- What support might they need academically or emotionally?
- What family rhythms and faith practices do you want to continue?

Talk with your children early and often about the move back.

📝 Reflect & Plan:

Transition with Intention
 Reflect
What might be emotionally difficult for your children during this season?

What routines or relationships helped them thrive overseas?

Are they excited? Nervous? A mix of both?

Plan
Calendar Planning: Mark key dates—travel, school, rest, mission visits, family time.

Talk About Expectations: Ask questions like:
 "What are you excited about?"
 "What might feel weird or hard?"
 "Who are you looking forward to seeing?"

Create a Safe Space: Prepare a spot (bedroom, study area) that offers comfort and predictability.

👪 Family Task: Reflecting Together

Story Mapping
Draw a timeline or map with your children showing the places you've lived, people you've met, and moments that stood out.

Emotion Sorting
Use feelings cards, colour codes, or drawings to help your child express:
- What was hard?
- What was fun?
- What do I want to remember?

Suitcase Reflection
Ask:
- "If you could pack one memory, one challenge, one lesson, and one wish—what would you take with you?"

Memory Box
Create a physical box with meaningful items from the field—photos, small gifts, keepsakes—to revisit during the home assignment.

Companion Activity

Create a Photo Book

✅ Key Takeaways

- Home assignment is an important and active part of your global life—not just a break.
- Debriefing allows children to process, heal, and understand their experience.
- Planning gives structure and reduces anxiety during a season that can feel unfamiliar.
- Your child may feel torn between joy and grief—give them space to hold both.
- Helping your family reflect well now will make re-entry smoother and build long-term resilience.

Section 18

Bonus Tools

Using Mood Trackers Before a Move

What Is a Mood Tracker?
A mood tracker is a simple tool that helps children identify and express how they're feeling day by day. As your family prepares to return to your passport country—or make any major transition—it can be difficult for kids to describe the mix of emotions they're experiencing. Mood trackers give them a visual, non-verbal way to process their inner world.

Why It Matters Before a Move
Leading up to a big change like home assignment, children often experience:
- Excitement and anxiety at the same time
- Sadness about leaving friends or routines
- Confusion about what's coming next
- Emotional outbursts or withdrawal without clear explanation

By tracking moods each day or week, children can:
- Begin naming and normalising their emotions
- Recognise patterns (e.g., "I feel better when I talk about it")
- Open the door to gentle conversations with you
- Build self-awareness and emotional vocabulary

How to Use a Mood Tracker
- Choose a format that fits your child: colour chart, emoji faces, sticker calendar, or a simple daily journal.
- Let them fill it in daily or a few times a week—no pressure to explain.

Use it as a springboard for connection:
"I noticed you marked today as a 'blue' day—want to tell me about it?"
"You've had lots of happy faces lately! What's been going well?"

- Blue- Sad
- Red- Angry
- Yellow – Happy
- Green- Anxious
- Orange- Worried
- Purple- Scared

Each family member to add their own code

The River: A Self-Reflection Tool for Your Transition Journey

As your family prepares to move overseas, you may find that everyone is processing the change differently. The River is a visual reflection tool designed to help you check in—both as individuals and as a family—about where you are in the transition process.

How It Works
Picture the journey like crossing a river:
- One side is where you live now—your current home, friends, routines, and comforts.
- The other side is your next destination—your new country, calling, or season of life.
- The river in between represents the transition itself. It's the space between the "known" and the "new."

Crossing this river looks different for each person. Some may be paddling ahead with excitement, others may feel like they're barely staying afloat. That's normal.

Use This Tool to Reflect as a Family
Take a moment to check in together:
- Where do I see myself in the river today?
- Am I excited, anxious, tired, or curious?
- What's helping me stay afloat—people, routines, faith, fun?
- Do I feel stuck or like I'm already reaching the other shore?
- Is anyone in our family moving at a different pace—and how can we support each other?

You can draw a picture of the river together or use printed river templates for each family member. Have them mark where they feel they are and explain (if they want) why they chose that spot.

Donovan (1991) A model of major transition

Section 19

Resources

Resource Page: Helpful Reads for Families Preparing to Move Overseas

These books offer insight, encouragement, and practical support for families navigating the challenges of cross-cultural life and raising Third Culture Kids (TCKs). Whether you're just starting your journey or actively preparing to move overseas, these resources can equip you along the way.

Core Reads on TCK Life and Global Transitions

- Misunderstood: The Impact of Growing Up Overseas in the 21st Century
Tanya Crossman (Summertime Publishing, 2016)
- Third Culture Kids: Growing Up Among Worlds (3rd Edition)
David Pollock, Ruth Van Reken, Michael Pollock (Nicholas Brealey Publishing, 2017)
- Third Culture Kids: A Gift to Care For Ulrika Ernvik (Familjeglädje, 2018)
- Raising a Generation of Healthy Third Culture Kids (Independently published, 2020)

Family Preparation & Transition

- Families on the Move Marion Knell (Monarch Books, 2001)
- Unstacking Your Grief Tower Lauren Wells (Independently published, 2021)
- Belonging Beyond Borders Megan Norton (Belonging Beyond Borders LLC, 2022)
- Between Worlds: Essays on Culture and Belonging Marilyn Gardner (Doorlight Publications, 2015)
- Worlds Apart: A Third Culture Kid's Journey Marilyn Gardner (Doorlight Publications, 2018)

Adventure Awaits

Adventure Awaits

Adventure Awaits

www.ingramcontent.com/pod-product-compliance
Lightning Source LLC
Chambersburg PA
CBHW081417300426
44109CB00020BA/2356